HISTORICAL COMMENTARY
ON THE OLD TESTAMENT

* * * *

EXODUS

T0166106

HISTORICAL COMMENTARY

ON THE OLD TESTAMENT

Editorial team:

Cornelis Houtman
(Kampen, The Netherlands)

Gert T.M. Prinsloo
(Pretoria, South Africa)

Wilfred G.E. Watson
(Newcastle, UK)

Al Wolters
(Ancaster, Ontario, Canada)

EXODUS

by

Cornelis Houtman

Volume 4

Supplement

PEETERS - LEUVEN

Houtman, C.
Exodus - Vol. 4.
(Historical Commentary on the Old Testament)
Cover design by Dick Prins
NUGI 632
ISBN 90-429-1126-3
D. 2002/0602/47

CONTENTS

PREFACE

The indexes in this supplement to my commentary on Exodus (Vol. 1, 1993; Vol. 2, 1996; Vol. 3, 2000) are designed to provide easier access to the wide range of subjects touched on than would be possible solely through consulting tables of contents. They are intended as starting points to put the user on the track of further information found in the many references in the text itself.

The index of Hebrew words and phrases contains an overview of almost all the terms used in Exodus. Omitted are prepositions and some pronouns and particles. Personal and geographical names are included in the index of subjects.

I took the opportunity to make many bibliographical additions, especially of recent literature.

In the indexes and bibliographical additions the numerals in regular type refer to the pages in Vol. 1 of the commentary, those in *italics* to Vol. 2, and those in **bold face** to Vol. 3.

Kampen, New-Year's Eve 2001   C. Houtman

INDEX TO SUBJECTS
Personal and geographical names included

INDEX TO HEBREW WORDS AND PHRASES

BIBLIOGRAPHICAL ADDITIONS

General literature

– A. Brenner (ed.), *Exodus to Deuteronomy* (The Feminist Companion to the Bible, Second Series), Sheffield 2000.
– H. Cazelles, *Autour de l'Exode*, Paris 1987 (collected essays 'about Exodus').
– D.J.A. Clines, "Images of Yahweh: God in the Pentateuch," in: R.L. Hubbard et al. (eds), *Studies in Old Testament Theology*, 79-98.
– G.W. Coats, *Exodus 1-18*, Grand Rapids, MI 1999.
– J.J. Collins, "The Exodus and Biblical Theology," in: A. Ogden Bellis, J.S. Kaminsky (eds.), *Jews, Christians, and the Theology of the Hebrew Scriptures*, Atlanta, GA 2000, 247-61.
– J.J. Collins, "Reinventing Exodus: Exegesis and Legends in Hellenistic Egypt," in: R.A. Argall et al. (eds), *For a Later Generation: The Transformation of Tradition in Israel, Early Judaism, and Early Christianity* (FS G.W.E. Nickelsburg), Harrisburg 2000, 52-62.
– G.I. Davies, "The Theology of Exodus," in: E. Ball (ed.), *In Search of True Wisdom: Essays in Old Testament Interpretation* (FS R.E. Clements), Sheffield 1999, 137-52.
– L. Eslinger, "Freedom or Knowledge? Perspective and Purpose in the Exodus Narrative (Exodus 1-15)," *JSOT* 52 (1991), 43-60.
– P. Enns, *Exodus* (The NIV Application Commentary), Grand Rapids 2000.
– G. Fischer, "Keine Priesterschrift in Ex 1-15?," *ZKTh* 117 (1995), 203-11.
– G. Fischer, "Exodus 1-15: Eine Erzählung," in: M. Vervenne (ed.), *Studies in the Book of Exodus*, Leuven 1996, 149-78.
– B.N. Fisk, "'One Good Story Deserves Another: The Hermeneutics of Invoking Secondary Biblical Episodes in the Narratives of *Pseudo-Philo* and the *Testaments of the Twelve Patriarchs*," in: C.A. Evans (ed.), *The Interpretation of Scripture in Early Judaism and Christianity: Studies in Language and Tradition*, Sheffield 2000, 217-38 [on Exod. 1-2; 14; 32; 34].
– T.E. Fretheim, *Exodus* (Interpretation), Louisville 1991.
– J.C. Gertz, *Tradition und Redaktion in der Exoduserzählung: Untersuchungen zur Endredaktion des Pentateuch*, Göttingen 2000.
– W. Groß, "Die Position des Subjekts im hebräischen Verbalsatz, untersucht an den asyndetischen ersten Redesätzen in Gen, Ex 1-19, Jos-2 Kön," *ZAH* 6 (1993), 170-87.
– D. Krochmalnik, *Schriftauslegung: Das Buch Exodus im Judentum*, Stuttgart 2000.

- W. Johnstone, *Chronicles and Exodus: An Analogy and its Application*, Sheffield 1998.
- J.D. Levenson, "Liberation Theology and the Exodus," in: A. Ogden Bellis, J.S. Kaminsky (eds.), *Jews, Christians, and the Theology of the Hebrew Scriptures*, Atlanta, GA 2000, 215-30.
- J.D. Levenson, "The Perils of Engaged Scholarship: A Rejoinder to Jorge Pixley," in: A. Ogden Bellis, J.S. Kaminsky (eds.), *Jews, Christians, and the Theology of the Hebrew Scriptures*, Atlanta, GA 2000, 239-46.
- J.D. Levenson, "The Exodus and Biblical Theology: A Rejoinder to John J. Collins," in: A. Ogden Bellis, J.S. Kaminsky (eds.), *Jews, Christians, and the Theology of the Hebrew Scriptures*, Atlanta, GA 2000, 263-75.
- J.A. Loader, "Exodus, Liberation Theology and the Theological Argument," *OTWSA* 29 (1986), 147-71.
- M.I. Lockshin (ed. and transl.), *Rashbam's Commentary on Exodus: An Annotated Translation*, Atlanta, GA 1997.
- A. Niccacci, "Yahveh e il Faraone: Teologia biblica ed egiziana a confronto," *BN* 38-39 (1987), 85-102.
- R. North, "Perspective of the Exodus Author(s)," *ZAW* 113 (2001), 481-504.
- E. Otto, "Die nachpriesterschriftliche Pentateuchredaktion im Buch Exodus," in: M. Vervenne (ed.), *Studies in the Book of Exodus*, Leuven 1996, 61-111.
- F. Petit, *La chaîne sur l'Exode: Édition integrale IV. Fonds caténique ancien (Exode 15,22-40,32)*, Leuven 2001.
- T.D. Proffitt, "The Exodus as a Revitalization Movement," *Folia Orientalia* 23 (1985-86), 237-44.
- J.V. Pixley, "History and Particularity in Reading the Hebrew Bible: A Response to Jon D. Levenson" in: A. Ogden Bellis, J.S. Kaminsky (eds.), *Jews, Christians, and the Theology of the Hebrew Scriptures*, Atlanta, GA 2000, 231-37.
- F. Polak, "Theophany and Mediator: The Unfolding of a Theme in the Book of Exodus," in: M. Vervenne (ed.), *Studies in the Book of Exodus*, Leuven 1996, 113- 47.
- W.H.C. Propp, *Exodus 1-18: A New Translation with Introduction and Commentary* (Anchor Bible), New York 1999.
- L.J. de Regt, "Aspects of the Syntax and Rhetoric of Participant Reference in Exodus," in: M. Vervenne (ed.), *Studies in the Book of Exodus*, Leuven 1996, 515-22.
- G. Sauer, "Vom Exoduserleben zur Landnahme: Theologische Erwägungen," *ZThK* 79 (1982), 26-32.
- R.S. Sugirtharajah (ed.), *Voices from the Margin: Interpreting the Bible in the Third World*, Maryknoll, NY 1991 (Part 3 [pp. 229-95] contains several approaches to the exodus).
- J.T. Townsend, *Midrash Tanḥuma: Translated into English with Indices and*

Brief Notes (S. Buber Recension) II. Exodus and Leviticus, Hoboken, NJ 1997.
- H. Utzschneider, "Die Renaissance der alttestamentlichen Literaturwissenschaft und das Buch Exodus: Überlegungen zu Hermeneutik und Geschichte der Forschung," *ZAW* 106 (1994), 197-223.
- M. Vervenne, "Current Tendencies and Developments in the Study of the Book of Exodus," in: M. Vervenne (ed.), *Studies in the Book of Exodus*, Leuven 1996, 21-59.
- W. Vogels, "D'Égypte à Canaan: Un rite de passage," *ScEs* 52 (2000), 21-35.

Additions to Volume 1

3   P. Cassuto, *Qere-Ketib et listes massoretiques dans le manuscript B 19a*, Frankfurt a.M. etc. 1989.
     A.A. Lieberman, "*lw/l*': An Analysis of a Kethib-Qere Phenomenon," in: E.J. Revell (ed.), *VIII International Congress of the International Organization for Masoretic Studies Chicago 1988*, Atlanta, GA 1990, 79-86.

10   G. Goldenberg, "On Direct Speech and the Hebrew Bible," in: K. Jongeling et al. (eds), *Studies in Hebrew and Aramaic Syntax* (FS J. Hoftijzer), Leiden etc. 1991, 79-96.
     S.A. Meier, *Speaking of Speaking: Marking Direct Discourse in the Hebrew Bible*, Leiden etc. 1992.
     W.C. van Wyk, "The Syntax of אשר in Biblical Hebrew Investigated Anew," *Jsem* 4 (1992), 200-9.

11   A. van der Lingen, "*bw'-yṣ*' ('To Go Out and To Come In') As a Military Term," *VT* 42 (1992), 59-66.
     J.-C. Petit (ed.), *'Où demeures-tu?': La maison depuis le monde biblique* (FS G. Couturier), Québec 1994.

12   S. Bendor, *The Social Structure of Ancient Israel: The Institution of the Family* (beit 'ab) *from the Settlement to the End of the Monarchy*, Jerusalem 1996.

15   W. Schneider, "Dabar bedeutet 's'," *BN* 58 (1991), 24-8.

16   W. Schneider, "Und es begab sich ...: Anfänge von Erzählungen im biblischen Hebräisch," *BN* 70 (1993), 62-87.

19   T. Zewi, "The Particles *hinnēh* and *wĕhinnēh* in Biblical Hebrew," *Hebrew Studies* 37 (1996), 21-38.

22   R. Dietzfelbinger, "Ego indurabo cor Pharaonis: Anmerkungen zu einer crux interpretum,": in R. Gryson (ed.), *Philologia Sacra: Biblische und patristische Studien für H.J. Wrede und W. Thiele zu ihrem siebzigsten Geburtstag*, I, Freiburg etc. 1993, 16-35.
     J. Krašovec, *Reward, Punishment, and Forgiveness: The Thinking and Beliefs of Ancient Israel in the Light of Greek and Modern Views*, Leiden etc. 1999, 56-76.
     H. Liss, "Die Funktion der 'Verstockung' Pharaos in der Erzählung vom

Auszug aus Ägypten (Ex 7-14)," *BN* 93 (1998), 56-76.

24 R. Koch, *Die Sünde im Alten Testament*, Frankfurt am Main etc. 1992.

28 R. Kieffer, J. Bergman (eds), *La main de Dieu = Die Hand Gottes*, Tübingen 1997.

S. Kreuzer, "Die Verwendung der Mächtigkeitsformel außerhalb des Deuteronomiums: Literarische und theologische Linien zu Jer, Ez, DtrG und P," *ZAW* 109 (1997), 188-207, 369-84.

30 J.L.T. Kok, "Whose Staff is It, Anyway?," *BN* 85 (1996), 17-21.

J.L.T. Kok, *The Sin of Moses and the Staff of God: A Narrative Approach*, Assen 1997.

I.N. Rashkow, "Oedipus Wrecks: Moses and God's Rod," in: T.K. Beal, D.M. Gunn (eds), *Reading Bibles, Writing Bodies: Identity and the Book*, London/New York 1996, 72-84. Also published in A. Brenner (ed.), *Exodus to Deuteronomy*, Sheffield 2000, 59-74

37 R. North, "Brain and Nerve in the Biblical Outlook," *Bib* 74 (1993), 577-97.

40 C.S. Leeb, *Away from the Father's House: The Social Location of na'ar and na'arah in Ancient Israel*, Sheffield 2000.

42 Z. Zevit, "Phoenician *nbš/npš* and Its Hebrew Semantic Equivalents," *Maarav* 5-6 (1990), 337-44.

45 U. Berges, "Die Knechte im Psalter: Ein Beitrag zu seiner Kompositionsgeschichte," *Bib* 81 (2000), 153-178.

B.G. Wright, "Δοῦλος and Παῖς as Translations of עבד: Lexical Equivalents and Conceptual Transformations," in: B.A. Taylor (ed.), *IX Congress of the International Organization for Septuagint and Cognate Studies, Cambridge, 1995*, Atlanta, GA 1997, 263-77

46 W.G.E. Watson, "The Unnoticed Word Pair 'eye(s)' // 'heart'," *ZAW* 101 (1989), 398-408.

51 C. Dohmen, "'Nicht sieht mich der Mensch und lebt' (Ex 33, 20): Aspekte der Gottesschau im Alten Testament," *JBT* 13 (1998), 31-51.

M.S. Smith, "'Seeing God' in the Psalms: The Background to the Beatific Vision in the Hebrew Bible," *CBQ* 50 (1988), 171-83.

J.M. Vincent, *Das Auge hört: Die Erfahrbarkeit Gottes im Alten Testament*, Neukirchen-Vluyn 1998.

57 E. Gaß, "Genus und Semantik am Beispiel von 'theologischen' *rûḥ*," *BN* 109 (2001), 45-55.

H. Schüngel-Straumann, *Rûaḥ bewegt die Welt: Gottes schöpferische Lebenskraft in der Krisenzeit des Exils*, Stuttgart 1992.

W. von Soden, "Der Genuswechsel bei *rûaḥ* und das grammatische Geschlecht in den semtischen Sprachen," *ZAH* 5 (1992), 57-63.

58 J. Ellington, "Send!", *BiTr* 45 (1994), 228-38.

59 J. Arambarri, *Der Wortstamm 'hören' im Alten Testament: Semantik und Syntax eines hebräischen Verbs*, Stuttgart 1990.

60   D.O. Edzard, "Zahlen, Zählen, und Messen im Gilgames-Epos," in: W. Groß et al. (eds), *Text, Methode und Grammatik* (FS W. Richter), St. Ottilien 1991, 57-66.

B.J. Oosterhoff, *Om de Schriften te openen*, Kampen 1987, 38-50 (on number symbolism).

A. Schimmel, *The Mystery of Numbers*, Oxford 1993.

S. Valler, "The Number Fourteen as a Litererary Device in the Babylonian Talmud," *JSJ* 26 (1995), 169-84.

63   R. Gradwohl, "Drei Tage und der dritte Tag," *VT* 47 (1997), 373-8.

P. Särkiö, "'The Third Man' – David's Heroes in 2 Sam 23,8-39," *SJOT* 7 (1993), 108-24.

64   A. Meinhold, "Vierfaches: Strukturprinzip und Häufigkeitsfigur in Prov 1-9," *BN* 33 (1985), 53-79.

67   W. Berg, "Siebenerreihen von Verben und Substantiven," *BN* 84 (1996), 11-5.

70   E.W. Davies, "A Mathematical Conundrium: The Problem of the Large Numbers in Numbers I and XXVI," *VT* 45 (1995), 449-69.

D.M. Fouts,"Another Look at Large Numbers in Assyrian Royal Inscriptions," *JNES* 53 (1994), 205-11.

D.M. Fouts, "A Defense of the Hyperbolic Interpretation of Large Numbers in the Old Testament," *JETS* 40 (1997), 377-87.

R. Heinzerling, "Bileams Rätsel: Die Zählung der Wehrfähigen in Numeri 1 und 26," *ZAW* 111 (1999), 404-15.

C.J. Humphreys, "The Number of People in the Exodus From Egypt: Decoding Mathematically the Very Large Numbers in Numbers I and XVI," *VT* 48 (1998), 196-213.

C.J. Humphreys, "The Numbers in the Exodus From Egypt: A Further Appraisal,"*VT* 3 (2000), 323-8.

M. McEntire, "A Response to Colin.J. Humphreys's, 'The Number of People in the Exodus From Egypt: Decoding Mathematically the Very Large Numbers in Numbers I and XVI'," *VT* 49 (1999), 262-4.

G.A. Rendsburg, "An Additional Note To Two Recent Articles on the Number of People in the Exodus from Egypt and the Large Numbers in Numbers I and XXVI," *VT* 51 (2001), 392-6.

D.W. Young, "The Influence of Babylonian Algebra on Longevity Among the Antediluvians," *ZAW* 102 (1990), 321-35.

71   S.C. Layton, *Archaic Features of Canaanite Personal Names in the Hebrew Bible*, Atlanta, GA 1990.

H. Marks, "Biblical Naming and Poetic Etymology," *JBL* 114 (1995), 21-42.

H. Rechenmacher, *Personennamen als theologische Aussagen: Die syntaktischen und semantischen Strukturen der satzhaften theophoren Personen-*

namen in der hebräischen Bibel, St. Ottilien 1997.

H. Rechenmacher, "Zur Theologie der bibelhebräischen Personennamen," *MThZ* 51 (2000), 151-60.

A. Reinhartz, '*Why Ask My Name?*' *Anonymity and Identity in Biblical Narrative*, Oxford 1998.

W. Reyburn, "Names in Genesis," *BiTr* 45 (1994), 416-9.

75   R.A. Harrisville, *The Figure of Abraham in the Epistles of St. Paul: In the Footsteps of Abraham*, San Francisco 1992.

K.-W. Tröger, "Abraham im Koran," *Theologische Versuche* 16 (1986), 23-36.

76   H. Bamberger, "Aaron: Changing Perspectives," *Jud* 42 (1993), 201-13.

M.M. Homan, "A Tensile Etymology for Aaron: 'ahărōn › 'ahălōn," *BN* 95 (1998), 21-2.

78   S. Weitzman, "Reopening the Case of the Suspiciously Suspended Nun in Judges," *CBQ* 61 (1999), 448-60.

79   L.H. Feldman, "Josephus' Portrait of Joshua," *HThR* 82 (1989), 351-76.

M. Görg, "Juda-Namensdeutung in Tradition und Etymologie," in: R. Bartelmus et al. (eds), *Konsequente Traditionsgeschichte* (FS K. Baltzer), Fribourg/Göttingen 1993, 79-87.

C. Schäfer-Lichtenberger, *Josua und Salomo: Eine Studie zu Authorität und Legitimität des Nachfolgers im Alten Testament*, Leiden etc. 1995.

80   L.H. Feldman, "Josephus' Portrait of Joseph," *RB* 99 (1992), 504-28.

M. Görg, "Wohin ist Josef? Weitere Anfragen anläßlich einer Spurensuche," *BN* 107-108 (2001), 15-21.

M. Niehoff, *The Figure of Joseph in Post-Biblical Jewish Literature*, Leiden etc. 1992.

81   J.R. Baskin, *Pharaoh's Counsellors: Job, Jethro and Balaam in Rabbinic and Patristic Tradition*, Chico, California 1983.

83   J. Kugel, "Levi's Elevation to the Priesthood in Second Temple Writings," *HThR* 86 (1993), 1-64.

86   J. Assmann, *Moses der Ägypter: Entzifferung einer Gedächtnisspur*, München 1998.

J. Assmann, *Moses the Egyptian: The Memory of Egypt in Western Monotheism*, Cambridge, MA/London 1998.

A.G. Auld, *Kings without Privilege: David and Moses in the Story of the Biblical Kings*, Edinburgh 1994.

R.J. Bernstein, *Freud and the Legacy of Moses*, Cambridge 1998.

D. Boyarin, "'An Imaginary and Desirable Converse': *Moses and Monotheism* as Family Romance," in: T.K. Beal, D.M. Gunn (eds), *Reading Bibles, Writing Bodies: Identity and the Book*, London/New York 1996,184-204.

M. Clark, "Biblical and Early Islamic Mose," in: E.E. Carpenter (ed.), *A*

Biblical Itinerary: In Search of Method, Form and Content (FS G.W. Coats), Sheffield 1997, 20-38.

E.M. Dörfuss, *Mose in den Chronikbüchern: Garant theokratischer Zukunftserwartung*, Berlin/New York 1994.

G. Fischer, "Das Mosebild der hebräischen Bibel," in: E. Otto (ed.), *Mose: Ägyten und das Alte Testament*, Stuttgart 2000, 84-120.

M. Gawlick, "Mose in Johannesevangelium," *BN* 84 (1996), 29-35.

M. Görg, "Mose – Name und Namenträger: Versuch einer historischen Annäherung," in: E. Otto (ed.), *Mose: Ägyten und das Alte Testament*, Stuttgart 2000, 17-42.

S. Marx, "Moses and Macchiavellism," *JAAR* 65 (1997), 551-71.

H. McKeating, "Ezekiel The 'Prophet Like Moses'?" *JSOT* 61 (1994), 97-109.

S.A. Nigosian, "Moses As They Saw Him," *VT* 43 (1993), 339-50.

J. Nohrberg, *Like unto Moses: The Constituting of an Interruption*, Bloomington/Indianapolis 1995.

E. Otto, "Mose und das Gesetz: Die Mose-Figur als Gegenentwurf politischer Theologie zur neuassyrischen Königsideologie im 7.Jh. v. Chr., " in: idem (ed.), *Mose: Ägyten und das Alte Testament*, Stuttgart 2000, 43-83.

M. O'Kane, "Isaiah: A Prophet in the Footsteps of Moses," *JSOT* 69 (1996), 29-51.

R. Rendtorff, "Some Reflections on the Canonical Moses: Moses and Abraham," in: E.E. Carpenter (ed.), *A Biblical Itinerary: In Search of Method, Form and Content* (FS G.W. Coats), Sheffield 1997, 11-9.

W.H. Schmidt, in: P. Antes (ed.), *Große Religionsstifter: Zarathustra, Mose, Jesus, Mani, Muhammad, Nanak, Buddha, Lao Zi*, München 1992, 32-48.

R. Smend, "Mose als geschichtliche Gestalt," *Historische Zeitschrift* 260 (1995), 1-19.

87 L.H. Feldman, "Josephus' Portrait of Moses," *JQR* 82-83 (1991-93), 7-50, 285-328.

R.A. Freund, "'Thou Shalt Not Go Thither': Moses and Aaron's Punishments and Varying Theodices in the MT, LXX and Hellenistic Literature," *SJOT* 8 (1994), 105-25.

S.J. Hafemann, "Moses in the Apocrypha and Pseudepigrapha: A Survey," *JSP* 7 (1990), 79-104.

J. van Hartingsveld, *Mozes als wetgever naar de beschrijving van Flavius Josephus in de Antiquitates boek II-IV*, Kampen 1994.

B.M. Wheeler, "Moses or Alexander? Early Islamic Exegesis of Qur'an 18, 60-65," *JNES* 57 (1998), 191-215.

M. Witte, "'Mose, sein Andenken sei zum Segen' (Sir 45,1) – Das Mosebild des Sirachbuchs," *BN* 107-108 (2001), 161-86.

A.Z. Zivotofsky, "The Leadership Qualities of Moses," *Judaism* 43 (1994), 258-69.

88   F.M. Cross, "Reuben, the Firstborn of Jacob: Sacral Traditions and Early Israelite History," in: idem, *From Epic to Canon: History and Literature in Ancient Israel*, Baltimore/London 2000, 151-72.

89   A. Brenner, "Who's Afraid of Feminist Criticism? Who's Afraid of Biblical Humour? The Case of the Obtuse Foreign Ruler in the Hebrew Bible," *JSOT* 63 (1994), 38-55 (on among others Pharaoh).
     W. Brueggemann, "Pharaoh as Vassal: A Study of a Political Metaphor," *CBQ* 57 (1195), 27-51.
     R.A. Friend, "Naming Names: Some Observations on 'Nameless Women' Traditions in the MT, LXX and Hellenistic Literature," *SJOT* 6 (1992), 213-32.

91   R. Rendtorff, "'*El* als israelitische Gottesbezeichnung. *Mit einem Appendix: Beobachtungen zum Gebrauch von* הָאֱלֹהִים.," *ZAW* 106 (1996), 4-21.

92   Y. Hoffman, "The Concept of 'Other Gods' in the Deuteronomistic Literature," in: H. Graf Reventlow (ed.), *Politics and Theopolitics in the Bible and Postbiblical Literature*, Sheffield 1994, 66-84.

94   J.P. Floss, "Ich bin mein Name: Die Identität von Gottes Ich und Gottes Namen nach Ex 3,14," in: W. Groß (ed.), *Text, Methode und Grammatik* (FS W. Richter), St. Ottilien 1991, 67-80.
     C. den Hertog, "Exodus 3:14 in de Septuaginta: 'Ik ben "der Zijnde"' – een metafysische uitspraak?" *NedThT* 53 (1999), 1-16.
     A. Ibáñez Arana, "Ex 3,14a, explicación de un nombre singular: YHWH," *EstBib* 57 (1999), 375-88.
     M. Rösel, "Theo-logie der griechischen Bibel: Zur Wiedergabe der Gottesaussagen im LXX-Pentateuch," *VT* 48 (1998), 49-62.

95   C. den Hertog, "De naam van de God van de profeten: Exodus 3:13-15," *ACEBT* 12 (1993), 38-61.
     C. den Hertog, "De godsnaam in Hosea 1:9: Een commentaar op Exodus 3:14?," *ACEBT* 17 (1999), 75-83.
     S.M. McDonough, *YHWH at Patmos: Rev. 1:4 in its Hellenistic and Early Jewish Setting*, Tübingen 1999 (the background of the divine name in the greeting of Rev. 1:4 is taken as a reflection on the divine name as revealed in Exod. 3:14).
     A. and L. Phillips, "The Origin of 'I Am' in Exodus 3.14," *JSOT* 78 (1998), 81-4.
     H. Irsigler, "Von der Namensfrage zum Gottesverständnis: Exodus 3,13-15 im Kontext der Glaubensgeschichte Israels," *BN* 96 (1999), 56-96.

98   J.A. Emerton, "'Yahweh and His Asherah': The Goddess or Her Symbol?," *VT* 49 (1999), 315-37.
     V. Fritz, "Jahwe und El in den vorpriesterlichen Geschichtswerken," in: I.

Kottsieper et al. (eds), *'Wer ist wie du, Herr, unter den Göttern?'* *Studien zur Theologie und Religionsgeschichte Israels* (FS O. Kaiser), Göttingen 1994, 111-26.

Th.L. Thompson, "How Yahweh Became God: Exodus 3 and 6 and the Heart of the Pentateuch," *JSOT* 68 (1995), 57-74.

99 J. Becker, "Zur 'Ich bin'-Formel im Alten Testament," *BN* 98 (1999), 45-54.

101 H. Lutzky, "Shadday as a Goddess Epithet," *VT* 48 (1998), 15-36.

102 C. Bailey, "Bedouin Place-Names in Sinai," *PEQ* 116 (1984), 42-57.

A. Vonach, "Der 'Exodus' – Physische Anstrengung oder geistige Leistung? Implikationen der Ortsnamen von Ex 1-15 auf die Entstehung und Bedeutung des Exodusbuches," *Protokolle zur Bibel* 9 (2000), 123-31.

103 J.R. Bartlett, *Edom and the Edomites*, Sheffield 1989.

B. Dicou, *Edom, Israel's Brother and Antagonist*, Sheffield 1994.

D.V. Edelman (ed.), *You Shall Not Abhor an Edomite for He is Your Brother: Edom and Seir in History and Tradition*, Atlanta, GA 1995.

B. MacDonald, *Ammon, Moab and Edom: Early States/Nations of Jordan in the Biblical Period*, Amman 1994.

110 J.R. Bartlett, "'Ezion-Geber, Which is Near Elath on the Shore of the Red Sea' (I Kings IX 26)," *OTS* 26 (1990), 1-16.

H. Lamberty-Zielinski, *Das 'Schilfmeer': Herkunft, Bedeutung und Funktion eines alttestamentlichen Exodusbegriffs*, Frankfurt am Main 1993.

M. Vervenne, "The Lexeme סוּף (*sûph*) and the Phrase יָם סוּף (*yam sûph*): A Brief Reflection on the Etymology and Semantics of a Key Word in the Hebrew Exodus Tradition," in: K. van Lerberghe, A. Schoors (eds), *Immigration and Emigration within the Ancient Near East* (FS E. Lipiński), Leuven 1995, 403-29.

112 N.P. Lemche, "City-Dwellers or Administrators: Further Light on the Canaanites," in: A. Lemaire, B. Otzen (eds), *History and Traditions of Early Israel* (FS E. Nielsen), Leiden etc. 1993, 76-89.

A.F. Rainey, "Who is a Canaanite? A Review of the Textual Evidence," *BASOR* 304 (1996), 1-15.

113 D.C. Benjamin, "Response to Paula M. McNutt: The Kenites, the Midianites, and the Rechabites," *Semeia* 67 (1994), 133-45.

P.M. McNutt, "The Kenites, the Midianites, and the Rechabites as Marginal Mediators in Ancient Israelite Tradition," *Semeia* 67 (1994), 109-32.

114 A. Dearmann (ed.), *Studies in the Mesha Inscription and Moab*, Atlanta, GA 1989.

115 M. Görg, *Die Beziehungen zwischen dem alten Israel und Ägypten*, Darmstadt 1997.

122 E. Anati, "Exodus et Sinai: Une reconsideration," in: A. Matthias, K.-D. Schunck, *'Dort ziehen Schiffe dahin...': Collected Communications to the*

42 EXODUS/SUPPLEMENT

XIVth Congress of the International Organization for the Study of the Old Testament, Paris 1992, Frankfurt etc. 1996, 11-25.

123 M.C. Astour, " The Ḫapiru in the Amarna Texts," *UF* 31 (1999), 31-50.

125 R. Drews, "Canaanites and Philistines," *JSOT* 81 (1998), 39-61.

T. and M. Dothan, *People of the Sea: The Search for the Philistines*, New York/Oxford 1992.

C.S. Ehrlich, *The Philistines in Transition: A History from ca. 1000-730 B.C.E.*, Leiden etc. 1996.

O. Margalith, "Where Did the Philistines Come From?" *ZAW* 107 (1995), 101-9.

H.M. Niemann, "Das Ende des Volkes der Perizziter. Über soziale Wandlungen Israels im Spiegel einer Begriffsgruppe," *ZAW* 105 (1993), 233-57.

130 B.J. Collins (ed.), *A History of the Animal World in the Ancient Near East*, Groningen 2001.

K.J. Dell, "The Use of Animal Imagery in the Psalms and Wisdom Literature of Ancient Israel," *SJTh* 53 (2000), 275-91.

E. Firmage, "Zoology," *ABD*, VI, 1109-67.

U. Hübner, *Spiele und Spielzeug im antiken Palästina*, Freiburg/Göttingen 1992 (on animals as playmates).

P. Riede, "'Denn wie der Mensch jedes Tier nennen würde, so sollte es heißen': Hebräische Tiernamen und was sie uns verraten," *UF* 25 (1993), 331-78.

R. Whitekettle, "Where the Wild Things Are: Primary Level Taxa in Israelite Zoological Thought," *JSOT* 93 (2001), 17-37.

131 B.A. Mastin, "What Do *Miqneh* and *Bᵉhēmâ* mean in Genesis xxxiv 23, xxxvi 6; Numbers xxxi 9, xxxii 26?" *VT* 45 (1995), 491-515.

R. Péter-Contesse, "Quels animaux Israël offrait-il en sacrifice?" in: A. Schenker (ed.), *Studien zu Opfer und Kult im Alten Israel*, Tübingrn 1992, 67-77.

132 K. Koenen, "'... denn wie der Mensch jedes Tier nennt, so soll es heißen' (Gen 2,19): Zur Bezeichnung von Rindern im Alten Testament," *Bib* 75 (1994), 539-46.

134 I. Köhler-Rollefson, "Camels and Camel Pastoralism in Arabia," *BA* 56 (1993), 180-8.

143 I.M. Ceccherelli, "La 'manne'," *BeO* 39 (1997), 56.

144 J. Wilkinson, "The Quail Epidemic of Numbers 11.31-34," *EvQ* 71 (1999), 195-208.

145 S. Dalley, "Hebrew *taḥaš*, Akkadian *duhšu*, Faience and Beadwork," *JSS* 45 (2000), 1-19.

M. Görg, "Das Lexem *taḥaš* – Herkunft und Bedeutung," *BN* 109 (2001), 5-9.

M. Stol, "Leder(industrie)," *RLA*, VI, 527-43.

146 B. Janowski et al. (eds), *Gefährten und Feinde des Menschen: Das Tier in der Lebenswelt des alten Israel*, Neukirchen-Vluyn 1993.

K. Koenen, "'Süßes geht vom Starken aus'(Ri 14,14): Vergleiche zwischen Gott und Tier im Alten Testament," *EvTh* 54 (1994), 174-97.

H.-P. Mathys (ed.), *Ebenbild Gottes – Herrscher über die Welt*, Neukirchen-Vluyn 1998.

F. Schmitz-Kahmen, *Geschöpfe Gottes unter den Obhut des Menschen: Die Wertung der Tiere im Alten Testament*, Neukirchen-Vluyn 1997.

R. Stahl, "'Alles setztest du ihm zu Füßen'," in: M. Albani, T. Arndt (eds), *Gottes Ehre erzählen* (FS H. Seidel), Leipzig 1994, 51-62.

E. Schwab, "Die Tierbilder und Tiervergleiche des Alten Testaments: Material und Problemanzeigen," *BN* 59 (1991), 37-43.

H.-J. Stipp, "'Alles Fleisch hatte seinen Wandel auf Erde verdorben' (Gen 6,12): Die Mitverantwortung der Tierwelt an der Sintflut nach der Priesterschrift," *ZAW* 111 (1999), 167-86.

148 J. Moorhead, "Cooking a Kid in Its Mother's Milk: Patristic Exegesis of an Old Testament Command," *Augustinianum* 37 (1997), 261-71.

150 I. and W. Jacob, "Flora," *ABD*, II, 803-17.

I. and W. Jacob (eds), *Pharmaceuticals in the Biblical and Rabbinical World*, Leiden etc. 1993.

154 R. Frankel, *Wine and Oil Production in Antiquity in Israel and Other Mediterranean Countries*, Sheffield 1999.

Th. C. de Kruijf, "Der Ölbaum und seine Frucht in der Kultur und im Kult des Altertums," *Bijdragen* 51 (1990), 246-56.

158 E. Lipiński, "Straw in the Neo-Assyrian Period," in: E. Wardini (ed.), *Built on Solid Rock* (FS E.E. Knudson), Oslo 1997, 187-95.

170 J. Kügler, "Gold, Weihrauch und Myrrhe: Eine notiz zu Mt 2,11," *BN* 87 (1997), 24-33.

172 P.R. Davies, *In Search of 'Ancient Israel'*, Sheffield 1992.

W.G. Dever, "The Identity of Early Israel: A Rejoinder to Keith W. Whitelam," *JSOT* 72 (1966), 3-24.

R. Drews, *The End of the Bronze Age: Changes in Warfare and the Catastrophe ca. 1200 B.C.*, Princeton 1993.

E.S. Frerichs, L.H. Lesko (eds), *Exodus: The Egyptian Evidence*, Winona Lake, IN 1997.

L.L. Grabbe, "*Adde praeputium praeputio magnus acervus erit*: If the Exodus and Conquest Had Really Happened," *BibInt* 8 (2000), 23-32.

S. Herrmann, "Observations on Some Recent Hypotheses Pertaining to Early Israelite History," in: H.G. Reventlow, Y. Hoffman (eds), *Justice and Righteousness: Biblical Themes and Their Influence*, Sheffield 1992, 105-16.

R.S. Hess, "Early Israel in Canaan: A Survey of Recent Evidence and Interpretation," *PEQ* 125 (1993), 125-42.

J.K. Hoffmeier, *Israel in Egypt: The Evidence for the Authenticity of the Exodus Tradition*, Oxford 1997.

D. Jericke, *Die Landnahme im Negev: Protoisraelitische Gruppen im Süden Palästinas: Eine archäologische und exegetische Studie*, Wiesbaden 1997.

S. Kreuzer, "Max Weber, George Mendenhall und das sogenannte Revolutionsmodelle für die 'Landnahme' Israels," in: P. Mommer, W. Thiel (eds.), *Altes Testament Forschung und Wirkung* (FS H. Graf Reventlow), Frankfurt am Main 1994, 283-305.

J.J. McDermott, *What Are They Saying About the Formation of Israel?*, New York/Mahwah 1998.

R.E. Muth, "Economic Influences on Early Israel," *JSOT* 75 (1997), 77-92.

R. Neu, *Von der Anarchie zum Staat: Entwicklungsgeschichte Israels vom Nomadentum zur Monarchie im Spiegel der Ethnosoziologie*, Neukirchen-Vluyn 1992.

K.L. Noll, "An Alternative Hypothesis for a Historical Exodus Event," *SJOT* 14 (2000), 260-74.

D.B. Redford, *Egypt, Canaan, and Israel in Ancient Times*, Princeton 1992.

H. Seebaß, "Dialog über Israels Anfänge: Zum Evolutionsmodell von N.P. Lemche, Early Israel," in: J. Hausmann, H.J. Zobel (eds), *Alttestamentliche Glaube und Biblische Theologie* (FS H.D. Preuß), Stuttgart etc. 1992, 11-9.

Th.L. Thompson, *Early History of the Israelite People: From the Written and Archaeological Sources*, Leiden etc. 1992.

K.W. Whitelam, "The Identity of Early Israel: The Realignment and Transformation of Late Bronze-Iron Palestine," *JSOT* 63 (1994), 57-87.

K.W. Whitelam, "Prophetic Conflict in Israelite History: Taking Sides with William G. Dever," *JSOT* 72 (1996), 57-87.

H.-J. Zobel, "'Israel' in Ägypten?" in: S. Kreuzer, K. Lüthi (eds), *Zur Aktualität des Alten Testaments* (FS G. Sauer), 1992, 109-17.

175 G.A. Rendsburg, "The Date of the Exodus and the Conquest/Settlement: The Case for the 1100S," *VT* 92 (1992), 510-27.

177 A. Nibbi, "Some Unanswered Questions on Canaan and Egypt and the So-Called Israel Stele," *BN* 73 (1994), 74-89 (cf. M. Görg, *BN* 74 [1994], 27).

K.W. Whitelam, "'Israel is Laid Waste; His Seed Is No More': What If Merneptah's Scribes Were Telling the Truth?," *BibInt* 8 (2000), 8-22.

188 M.D. Koster, "The Historicity of the Bible: Its Relevance and Its Limitations in the Light of Near Eastern Archaeology – From Catalyst to Cataclysm," *OTS* 44 (2000), 120-49.

A.R. Millard et al. (eds), *Faith, Tradition, and History: Old Testament Historiography in Its Near Eastern Context*, Winona Lake, IN 1994.

M.D. Oblath, "Of Pharaohs and Kings – Whence the Exodus?" *JSOT* 87 (2000), 23-42.

J. le Roux, "Israel's Past and the Feeling of Loss (Or: Deconstructing the 'Minimum' if the 'Minimalists' Even Further)," *OTE* 11 (1998), 477-86.

P. Särkiö, *Exodus und Salomo: Erwägungen zur verdeckten Salomokritik anhand von Ex 1-2; 5; 14 und 32*, Göttingen 1998.

Th.L. Thompson, *The Bible in History: How Writers Create a Past*, London 1999.

190   M. Dietmar, *Die Geschichtstheologie der Geschichtssummarien in den Psalmen*, Frankfurt etc. 1993.

A. Frisch, "The Exodus Motif in 1 Kings 1-14," *JSOT* 87 (2000), 3-21.

T. Hieke, "Der Exodus in Psalm 80: Geschichtstopik in den Psalmen," in: M. Vervenne (ed.), *Studies in the Book of Exodus*, Leuven 1996, 551-58.

V. Pröbstl, *Nehemia 9, Psalm 106 und Psalm 136 und die Rezeption des Pentateuch*, Göttingen 1997.

U. Schwenk-Bressler, *Sapientia Salomonis als ein Beispiel frühjudischer Textauslegung: Die Auslegung des Buches Genesis, Exodus 1-15 und Teilen der Wüstentradition in Sap 10-19*, Frankfurt etc. 1993.

A. van der Wal, "Themes from Exodus in Jeremiah 30-31," in: M. Vervenne (ed.), *Studies in the Book of Exodus*, Leuven 1996, 559-66.

192   S. Cheon, *The Exodus Story in the Wisdom of Solomon: A Study in Biblical Interpretation*, Sheffield 1997.

P. Enns, *Exodus Retold: Ancient Exegesis of the Departure from Egypt in Wis 10:15-21 and 19:1-9*, Atlanta, GA 1997.

196   A.R. Ceresko, "The Rhetorical Strategy of the Fourth Servant Song (Isaiah 52:13-53:12): Poetry and the Exodus–New Exodus," *CBQ* 56 (1994), 42-55.

S. Deck, "Kein Exodus bei Jesaja?" in: F. Diedrichs, B. Willmes (eds), *Ich bewirke das Heil und erschaffe das Unheil (Jesaja 45,7): Studien zur Botschaft der Propheten* (FS L. Ruppert), Würzburg 1998, 31-47.

R.E. Watts, *Isaiah's New Exodus and Mark*, Tübingen 1997.

208   L.C. Allen, "The Structuring of Ezekiel's Revisionist History Lesson (Ezekiel 20:3-31)," *CBQ* 54 (1992), 448-62.

R. Bartelmus, "Menschlicher Mißerfolg und Jahwes Initiative: Beobachtungen zum Geschichtsbild des deuteronomistischen Rahmens im Richterbuch und zum geschichtstheologischen Entwurf in Ez 20," *BN* 70 (1993), 28-47.

C. Patton, "'I Myself Gave Them Laws That Were Not Good': Ezekiel 20 and the Exodus Tradition," *JSOT* 69 (1996), 73-90.

K.P. Darr, "Ezekiel's Justifications of God: Teaching Troubling Texts," *JSOT* 55 (1992), 97-117.

211   S.E. Loewenstamm, *The Evolution of the Exodus Tradition*, Jerusalem 1992.

212   R.T. Anderson, "The Use of Hebrew Scriptures in Stephen's Speech," in: L.M. Hopfe (ed.), *Uncovering Ancient Stones: Essays in Memory of H. Neil*

Richardson, Winona Lake, IN 1994, 205-15.

R.B. Hays, *Echoes of Scripture in the Letters of Paul*, New Haven/London 1989

W. Kraus, "Johannes und das Alte Testament: Überlegungen zum Umgang mit der Schrift im Johannesevangelium im Horizont Biblischer Theologie," *ZNW* 88 (1997), 1-23.

B.G. Schuchard, *Scripture within Scripture: The Interrelationship of Form and Function in the Explicit Old Testament Citations in the Gospel of John*, Atlanta, GA 1992.

J.M. Scott, *Adoption as Sons of God: An Exegetical Investigation into the Background of HUIOTHESIA in the Pauline Corpus*, Tübingen 1992.

G.J. Steyn, *Septuagint Quotations in the Context of the Petrine and Pauline Speeches of the Acta Apostolorum*, Kampen 1995.

W.J. Webb, *Returning Home: New Covenant and Second Exodus as the Context for 2 Corinthians*, Sheffield 1993.

225 J.C. Exum, "Second Thoughts about Secondary Characters: Women in Exodus 1.8-2.10," in: A. Brenner (ed.), *A Feminist Companion to Exodus to Deuteronomy*, Sheffield 1994, 75-87.

E. Fuchs, "A Jewish-Feminist Reading of Exodus 1-2," in: A. Ogden Bellis, J.S. Kaminsky (eds.), *Jews, Christians, and the Theology of the Hebrew Scriptures*, Atlanta, GA 2000, 307-26.

P. Weimar, "Exodus 1,1-2,10 als Eröffnungskomposition des Exodusbuches," in: M. Vervenne (ed.), *Studies in the Book of Exodus*, Leuven 1996, 179-208.

227 Z. Kallai, "The Twelve-Tribe Systems of Israel", *VT* 47 (1997), 53-90.

243 H. Rösel, "Zur Bedeutung der Stadt im alttestamentlichen Israel", *BN* 89 (1997), 22-6.

251 P. Galpaz-Feller, "Pregnancy and Birth in the Bible and Ancient Egypt (Comparative Study)," *BN* 102 (2000), 42-53.

A. Kunz, "Die Vorstellung von Zeugung und Schwangerschaft im Antiken Israel," *ZAW* 111 (1999), 561-82.

M. Stol, *Birth in Babylonia and the Bible: Its Mediterranean Setting*, Groningen 2000, 118-24.

254 T. Römer, "Les sages-femmes du Pharaon et la 'crainte de Dieu' (Exode 1,15-22)," in: A. Matthias, K.-D. Schunck, *'Dort ziehen Schiffe dahin...': Collected Communications to the XIVth Congress of the International Organization for the Study of the Old Testament, Paris 1992*, Frankfurt etc. 1996, 183-90.

255 R.T. Hyman, "Fielding 'Why' Questions in Genesis," *HAR* 11 (1987), 173-83.

256 J. Siebert-Hommes, "Hebräerinnen sind חיות, "in: A. Matthias, K.-D. Schunck, *'Dort ziehen Schiffe dahin...': Collected Communications to the*

XIVth Congress of the International Organization for the Study of the Old Testament, Paris 1992, Frankfurt etc. 1996, 191-9.

257 R.J. Weems, "The Hebrew Women are not Like the Egyptian Women: The Ideology of Race, Gender and Sexual Reproduction in Exodus 1," *Semeia* 59 (1992), 25-34.

258 O. Horn Prouser, "The Truth about Women and Lying," *JSOT* 61 (1994), 15-28.

259 S.M. Paul, "Exodus 1:21: 'To Found a Family' – A Biblical and Akkadian Idiom," *Maarav* 8 (1992), 143-59.

268 M.C. Lee, "Genocide's Lament: Moses, Pharaoh's Daughter, and the Former Yugoslavia," in: T. Linafelt, T.K. Beal (eds), *God in the Fray* (FS W. Brueggemann), Minneapolis 1998, 66-82.

272 J. Ebach, "Die Schwester des Mose: Anmerkungen zu einem 'Widerspruch' in Exodus 2,1-10," in: idem, *Hiobs Post: Gesammelte Aufsätze zum Hiobbuch, zu Themen biblischer Theologie und zur Methodik der Exegese*, Neukirchen-Vluyn 1995, 130-44.

286 K. Engelken, *Frauen im Alten Israel*, Stuttgart etc. 1990, 330 (on 'girl').

289 L.-J. Bord, "L'adoption dans la Bible et dans le droit cunéiforme," *ZABR* 3 (1997), 174-94.
H.M. Wahl, "Ester, das adoptierte Waisenkind: Zur Adption im Alten Testament," *Bib* 80 (1999), 78-99.

299 P. Swiggers, "Nominal Sentence Negation in Biblical Hebrew: The Grammatical Status of אין," in: K. Jongeling et al. (eds), *Studies in Hebrew and Aramaic Syntax* (FS J. Hoftijzer), Leiden etc. 1991, 173-9.

301 J. M.G. Barclay, "Manipulating Moses: Exodus 2.10-15 in Egyptian Judaism and the New Testament," in: R.P. Carroll (ed.), *Text and Pretext: Essays in Honour of Robert Davidson*, Sheffield 1992, 28-46 (on the interpretation of Exod. 2:10-15 in the LXX, Artapanus, Ezekiel the Tragedian, Philo, Acts and Hebrews).

306 S. Bucher-Gillmayr, "Begegnungen am Brunnen," *BN* 75 (1994), 48-66.

307 R.A. Henshaw, *Female and Male: The Cultic Personnel: The Bible and the Rest of the Ancient Near East*, Allison Park, PA 1994.
P.J. Leithart, "Attendants of Yahweh's House: Priesthood in the Old Testament," *JSOT* 85 (1999), 3-24.
J.G. McConville, "Priesthood in Joshua to Kings," *VT* 49 (1999), 73-87.
K. Watanabe (ed.), *Priests and Officials in the Ancient Near East: Papers of the Second Colloquium on the Ancient Near East – The City and its Life held at the Middle Eastern Culture Center in Japan (Mitaka, Tokyo) March 22-24, 1996*, Heidelberg 1999.

313 A. Brenner, J.W. van Henten, "Food and Drink in the Bible: An Exciting New Theme," in: J.W. Dyk et al. (eds), *Unless Some One Guide Me...* (FS K.A. Deurloo), Maastricht 2001, 347-54.

J.-J. Glassner, "L'hospitalité en Mésopotamie ancienne: aspect de la question de l'étranger," *ZA* 80 (1990), 60-75.

T.R. Hobbs, "Hospitality in the First Testament and the 'Teleological Fallacy'," *JSOT* 95 (2001), 3-30.

A. Da Silva, "La symbolique du repas en Proche-Orient ancien," *SR* 24 (1995), 147-57.

314 M. Maher, "Targum Pseudo-Jonathan of Exodus 2.21," in: K.J. Cathcart, M. Maher (eds), *Targumic and Cognate Studies: Essays in Honour of Martin McNamara*, Sheffield 1996, 81-99.

316 R. Feldmeier, *Die Christen als Fremde: Die Metapher der Fremde in der antiken Welt, im Urchristentum und im 1. Petrusbrief*, Tübingen 1992.

G.G. Porton, *The Stranger within Your Gates: Converts and Conversion in Rabbinic Literature*, Chicago 1994.

F.A. Spina, "Israelites as *gērîm*, 'Sojourners,' in Social and Historical Context," in: C.L. Meyers, M. O'Connor (eds), *The Word of the Lord Shall Go Forth* (FS D.N. Freedman), Winona Lake, IN 1983, 321-35.

W. Vogels, "L'immigrant dans la maison d'Israël," in: J.-C. Petit (ed.), *'Où demeures/tu?' (Jn 1,38): La maison depuis le monde biblique* (FS G. Couturier), Québec 1994, 227-44.

323 R.P. Carroll, "Strange Fire: Abstract of Presence Absent in the Text: Meditations of Exodus 3," *JSOT* 61 (1994), 39-58.

327 P. Auffret, "A Poem in Prose: The Burning Bush Passage – Structural Analysis of Ex. 3:2-6," in: J.C. de Moor, W.G.E. Watson (eds), *Verse in Ancient Near Eastern Prose*, Neukirchen-Vluyn 1993, 1-12.

K. Berge, *Reading Sources in a Text: Coherence and Literary Criticism in the Call of Moses; Models –Methods –Micro-Analysis*, St. Ottilien 1997.

A.G. van Daalen, "The Place Where YHWH Showed Himself to Moses: A Study of the Composition of Exodus 3," in: M. Kessler (ed.), *Voices from Amsterdam*, Atlanta, GA 1994, 133-44.

J.-D. Macchi, "Exode et Vocation (Exode 3/1-12)," *EThR* 71 (1996), 67-74.

C. Seitz, "The Call of Moses and the 'Revelation' of the Divine Name: Source-Critical Logic and Its Legacy,": in C. Seitz et al. (eds), *Theological Exegesis* (FS B.S. Childs), Grand Rapis, MI/Cambridge, U.K. 1999, 145-67.

328 J. Day, "The Pharaoh of the Exodus, Josephus and Jubilees," *VT* 45 (1995), 377-8.

331 M.E. Andrew, "Bund und Land," in: P. Mommer et al. (eds), *Gottes Recht und Lebensraum* (FS H.J. Boecker), Neukirchen-Vluyn 1993, 131-44.

W. Groß, *Zukunft für Israel: Alttestamentliche Bundeskonzepte und die aktuelle Debatte um den neuen Bund*, Stuttgart 1998.

S. Van Den Eynde, "Covenant Formula and ברית: The Link between a Hebrew Lexeme and a Biblical Concept," *OTE* 12 (1999), 122-48.

J.-G. Heintz, "Alliance humaine – Alliance divine: Documents d'époque babylonienne ancienne & Bible hébraïque. – Une esquisse –," *BN* 86 (1997), 66-76.

N. Lohfink, "Bund als Vertrag im Deuteronomium," *ZAW* 107 (1995), 215-39.

B. Wodecki, "Les aspects sotériologiques de l'Alliance sinaïtique," in: A. Matthias, K.-D. Schunck, *'Dort ziehen Schiffe dahin...': Collected Communications to the XIVth Congress of the International Organization for the Study of the Old Testament, Paris 1992*, Frankfurt etc. 1996, 211-9.

M. Weinfeld, "Covenant Making in Anatolia and Mesopotamia," *JANES* 22 (1993), 135-9.

E. Zenger, *Der Neue Bund im Alten: Studien zur Bundestheologie der beiden Testamente*, Freiburg etc. 1993.

333 E. Bosetti, *Yahweh, Shepherd of the People: Pastoral Symbolism in the Old Testament*, Middlegreen/Mayhood 1993.

335 R. Bartelmus, "Begegnung in der Fremde: Anmerkungen zur theologischen Relevanz der topographischen Verortung der Berufungsvisionen des Mose und des Ezechiel (Ex 3,1-4,17 bzw. Ez 1,1-3,15)," *BN* 78 (1995), 21-38.

343 B.P. Robinson, "Moses at the Burning Bush," *JSOT* 75 (1997), 107-22.

359 H. Ausloos, "'A Land Flowing with Milk and Honey': Indicative of a Deuteronomist Redaction?," *EThL* 75 (1999), 297-314.

B.R. Knipping, "Die Wortkombination 'Land, fließend Milch und Honig': Eine kurze Problematisierung ihrer Ausdeutung, ihrer Überlieferungsgeschichte und der Tragweite eines Pentateuchmodells," *BN* 89 (1999), 55-71.

E. Levine, "The Land of Milk and Honey," *JSOT* 87 (2000), 43-57.

E. Levine, "The Promised Land of Milk and Honey," *EstBib* 58 (2000), 145-66.

363 W. Johnstone, "The Deuteronomistic Cycles of 'Signs' and 'Wonders' in Exodus 1-13," in: A. G. Auld, *Understanding Poets and Prophets* (FS G.W. Anderson), Sheffield 1993, 166-85.

364 C. den Hertog, "Concerning the Sign of Sinai (Ex. 3:12): Including a Survey of Prophetic and Call Signs," in: J.W. Dyk et al. (eds), *Unless Some One Guide Me...* (FS K.A. Deurloo), Maastricht 2001, 33-41.

369 J.L. Ska, "Récit et récit métadiégétique en Ex 1-15: Remarques critiques et essai d'interprétation de Ex 3,16-22," in: P. Haudebert (ed.), *Le Pentateuque: Débats et recherches*, Paris 1992, 135-71.

374 M.P. Zehnder, *Wegmetaphorik im Alten Testament*, Berlin/New York 1999.

378 P. Addinall, "Exodus III 19b and the Interpretation of Biblical Narrative," *VT* 49 (1999), 292-300.

J.L. Ska, "Note sur la traduction de *welō'* en Exode III 19b," *VT* 44 (1994), 60-5.

383 R. Gradwohl, "*Niṣṣal* und *hiṣṣîl* als Rechtsbegriffe im Sklavenrecht," *ZAW*

111 (1999), 187-95.

386 N.L. Collins, "Evidence in the Septuagint of a Tradition in Which the Is-
     raelites Left Egypt without Pharaoh's Consent," *CBQ* 56 (1994), 442-8.

395 R.C. Bailey, "'They Shall Become as White as Snow': When Bad is Turned
     into Good," *Semeia* 76 (1996), 99-113.

     N. Kiuchi, "A Paradox of the Skin Disease," *ZAW* 113 (2001), 505-14.

400 V. Haas, "Ein hurritischer Blutritus und die Deponierung der Ritu-
     alrückstände nach hethitischen Quellen," in: B. Janowski et al. (eds), *Reli-*
     gionsgeschichtliche Beziehungen zwischen Kleinasien, Nordsyrien und dem
     Alten Testament, Freiburg/Göttingen 1993, 66-85.

     M. Vervenne, "'The Blood is the Life and the Life is the Blood': Blood as
     Symbol of Life and Death in Biblical Tradition (Gen 9,4)," in: J. Quae-
     gebeur (ed.), *Ritual and Sacrifice in the Ancient Near East*, Leuven 1993,
     451-70.

406 M.J. Mulder, "Die Partikel אִ im biblischen Hebräisch," in: K. Jongeling et
     al. (eds), *Studies in Hebrew and Aramaic Syntax* (FS J. Hoftijzer), Leiden
     etc. 1991, 132-42.

408 L. Holden, *Forms of Deformity*, Sheffield 1991.

     V. Hurovitz, "Isaiah's Impure Lips and Their Purification in Light of Mouth
     Purification and Mouth Purity in Akkadian Sources," *HUCA* 40 (1989), 39-
     89.

411 D. Sivan, W. Schniedewind, "Letting Your 'Yes' Be 'No' in Ancient Israel:
     A Study of the Asseverative לֹא and הֲלֹא," *JSS* 38 (1993), 209-26.

412 S.B. Chapman, "'The Law and the Words' as a Canonical Formula within
     the Old Testament," in: C.A. Evans (ed.), *The Interpretation of Scripture in*
     Early Judaism and Christianity: Studies in Language and Tradition, Shef-
     field 2000, 26-74.

415 B.E. Baloian, *Anger in the Old Testament*, New York etc. 1992.

     P.A. Kruger, "A Cognitive Interpretation of the Emotion of Anger in the
     Hebrew Bible," *JNSL* 26 (2000), 181-93.

     K. Latvus, *God, Anger and Ideology: The Anger of God in Joshua and Jud-*
     ges in Relation to Deuteronomy and the Priestly Writings, Sheffield 1998.

429 E.W. Davies, "The Inheritance of the First-born in Israel and the Ancient
     Near East," *JSS* 38 (1993), 175-91.

     F.W. Golka, "Bechorah und Berachah: Erstgeburtsrecht und Segen," in: S.
     Beyerle et al. (eds), *Recht und Ethos im Alten Testament – Gestalt und*
     Wirkung (FS H. Seebass), Neukirchen-Vluyn 1991, 133-54.

     F.E. Greenspahn, *When Brothers Dwell Together: The Preeminence of*
     Younger Siblings in the Hebrew Bible, Oxford 1994.

     G.N. Knoppers, "The Preferential Status of the Eldest Son Revoked?", in:
     S.L. McKenzie, Th. Römer (eds), *Rethinking the Foundations: Histor-*
     iography in the Ancient World and in the Bible (FS J. Van Seters), Ber-

lin/New York 2000), 115-26.

432 B.J. Diebner, "'... und sie berührte ...': Zur 'Mitte' von Ex 4,24-26," *DBAT* 29 (1998), 96-8.

S. Frolov, "The Hero as Bloody Bridegroom: On the Meaning and Origin of Exodus 4.26," *Bib* 77 (1996), 520-3.

H.-C. Goßmann, "Metamorphosen eines Dämons: Ein Beitrag zur Rezeptionsgeschichte von Ex 4,24-26," in: D.-A. Koch, H. Lichtenberger (eds), *Begegnungen zwischen Christentum und Judentum in Antike und Mittelalter* (FS H. Schreckenberg), Göttingen 1993, 123-32.

S.D. Kunin, "The Bridegroom of Blood: A Structuralist Analysis," *JSOT* 70 (1996), 3-16.

W.H. Propp, "That Bloody Bridegroom (Exodus IV 24-26)," *VT* 43 (1993), 495-518.

H.-F. Richter, "Gab es einen 'Blutbräutigam'? Erwägungen zu Ex 4,24-26," in: M. Vervenne (ed.), *Studies in the Book of Exodus*, Leuven 1996, 433-41.

449 J. Goldingay, "The Significance of Circumsion," *JSOT* 88 (2000), 3-18.

465 P.J. King, "Warfare in the Ancient Near East," in: L.E. Stager et al. (eds), *The Archaeology of Jordan and Beyond* (FS J.A. Sauer), Winona Lake, IN 2000, 266-76.

495 B. Gosse, "Le souvenir de l'alliance avec Abraham, Isaac et Jacob et le serment du don de la terre dans la rédaction du Pentateuque," *EstBib* 51 (1993), 459-72.

B. Gosse, "Exode 6,8 comme réponse à Ezéchiel 33,24," *RHPhR* 74 (1994), 241-7.

B. Gosse, "Les premiers chapitres du livre de l'Exode et l'unification de la rédaction du Pentateuque," *BN* 86 (1997), 31-5.

B. Gosse, "Le livre d'Ezéchiel et Ex 6,2-8 dans le cadre du Pentateuque," *BN* 104 (2000), 20-5.

J. Lust, "Exodus 6,2-8 and Ezekiel," in: M. Vervenne (ed.), *Studies in the Book of Exodus*, Leuven 1996, 209- 24.

I.B. Gottlieb, "Law, Love, and Redemption: Legal Connotations in the Language of Exodus 6:6-8," *JANES* 26 (1998), 47-57.

511 A. Marx, " La généalogie d'Exode VI 14-25: Sa forme, sa function," *VT* 45 (1995), 318-36.

518 W. Adler, "Exodus 6:23 and the High Priest from the Tribe of Judah," *JTS* 48 (1997), 24-47.

530 J.D. Currid, "The Egyptian Setting of the 'Serpent' Confrontation in Exodus 7, 8-13," *BZ* 39 (1995), 203-24.

B.E. Scolnic, *Theme and Context in Biblical Lists*, Atlanta, GA 1995.

Additions to Volume 2

10 B. Lemmelijn, "'Zoals het nog nooit was geweest en ook nooit meer zou zijn' (Ex 11,6): De 'plagen van Egypte' volgens Ex 7-11: Historiciteit en theologie," *TvT* 36 (1996), 115-31.

B. Lemmelijn, "Transformations in Biblical Studies: The Story of the History of Research into the 'Plague Narrative' in Exod 7:14-11:10," *JNSL* 22 (1996), 117-27.

B. Lemmelijn, "As Many Texts as Plagues: A Preliminary Report of the Main Results of the Text-Critical Evaluation of Exod 7:14-11:10," *JNSL* 24 (1998), 111-25.

S.B. Noegel, "Moses and Magic: Notes on the Book of Exodus," *JANES* 24 (1996), 45-59.

W.H. Schmidt, "Die Intention der beiden Plagenerzählungen (Exodus 7-10) in ihrem Kontext," in: M. Vervenne (ed.), *Studies in the Book of Exodus*, Leuven 1996, 225-43.

E. Tov, "The Exodus Section of 4Q422," *Dead Sea Discoveries* 1 (1994), 197-209.

K.H. Walkenhorst, "Gotteserfahrung und Gotteserkenntnis: Im Sinne der priesterschriftlichen Redaktion von Ex 7-14," in: F.V. Reiterer (ed.), *Ein Gott – Eine Offenbarung: Beiträge zur biblischen Exegese, Theologie und Spiritualität* (FS N. Füglister), Würzburg 1991, 373-95.

36   B. Lemmelijn, "The Phrase ובעצים ובאבנים in Exodus 7,19," *Bib* 80 (1999), 264-8.

44   J.W. Rogerson, "Frontiers and Borders in the Old Testament," in: E. Ball (ed.), *In Search of True Wisdom* (FS R.E. Clements), Sheffield 1999, 116-26.

52   I. Himbaza, "La troisième et la qautrième plaies d'Égypte," *BN* 94 (1998), 68-78.

56   G.A. Klingbeil, "The *Finger of God* in the Old Testament," *ZAW* 112 (2000), 409-15.

107   M. O'Connor, "Biblical Hebrew Lexicography: טף 'children, dependents' in Biblical and Qumranic Hebrew," *JNSL* 25 (1999), 25-40.

115   B. Lemmelijn, "Setting and Function of Exod 11,1-10 in the Exodus Narrative," in: M. Vervenne (ed.), *Studies in the Book of Exodus*, Leuven 1996, 443-60.

146   D. Bergant, "An Anthropological Approach to Biblical Interpretation: The Passover Supper in Exodus 12:1-20 as a Case Study," *Semeia* 67 (1994), 43-62.

D. Büchner, "On the Relationship between *Mekhilta de Rabbi Ishmael* and Septuagint Exodus 12-23," in: B.A. Taylor (ed.), *IX Congress of the International Organization for Septuagint and Cognate Studies, Cambridge, 1995*, Atlanta, GA 1997, 403-20.

J. Jacobsen Buckley, "Response to Dianne Bergant: A Matter of Urgency," *Semeia* 67 (1994), 63-71.

J.G. McConville, "Deuteronomy's Unification of Passover and Maṣṣôt: A Response to Bernard M. Levinson," *JBL* 199 (2000), 47-58.

T. Prosic, "Passover in Biblical Narratives," *JSOT* 82 (1999), 45-55.

P. Weimar, "Exodus 12,24-27a: Ein Zusatz nachdeuteronomistischer Provenienz aus der Hand der Pentateuchredaktion," in: M. Vervenne, J. Lust (eds), *Deuteronomy and Deuteronomic Literature* (FS C.H.W. Brekelmans), Leuven 1997, 421-48.

160 G. Brin, *Studies in Biblical Law*, Sheffield 1994, 104-13 (on the law of Passover in the Temple Scroll).

E. Gaß, "Der Passa-Papyrus (Cowl 21¹) – Mythos oder Realität?" *BN* 99 (1999), 55-68.

162 G. Brin, *Studies in Biblical Law*, Sheffield 1994, 165-281 (on the laws of the first-born).

D.D. Hughes, *Human Sacrifice in Ancient Greece*, London 1991.

J. Van Seters, "The Law on Child Sacrifice in Exod 22,28b-29," *EThL* 74 (1998), 364-72

164 K. Koch, "Molek Astral," in: A. Lange et al. (eds.), *Mythos im Alten Testament und seiner Umwelt* (FS H.-P. Müller), Berlin/New York 1999, 29-50.

168 D.J.A. Clines, "The Evidence for an Autumnal New Year in Pre-exilic Israel Reconsidered," in: idem, *On the Way to the Postmodern: Old Testament Essays, 1967-1998*, 1, Sheffield 1998, 371-94

183 D. Büchner, "פסח: Pass Over or Protect?", *BN* 86 (1997), 14-7.

M.G. Kline, "The Feast of Cover-Over," *JETS* 37 (1994), 497-510.

210 M. Zehetbauer,"*Barmherzigkeit* als Lehnübersetzung: Die Etymologie des Begriffes im Hebräischen, Griechischen, Lateinischen und Deutschen – eine kleine Theologiegeschichte," *BN* 90 (1997), 67-83.

235 Th. Krüger, "Erwägungen zur Redaktion der Meerwundererzählung (Exodus 13,17-14,31)," *ZAW* 108 (1996), 519-33.

M. Vervenne, "Exodus Expulsion and Exodus Flight: The Interpretation of a Crux Critically Examined," *JNSL* 22 (1996), 45-58.

M. Vervenne, "Le récit de la mer (Exode xiii 17-xiv 31) reflète-t-il une rédaction de type deutéronomique? Quelques remarques sur le problème de l'identification des éléments deutéronomiques contenus dans le Tétrateuque," in: J.A. Emerton (ed.), *Congress Volume Cambridge 1995*, Leiden etc. 1997, 365-80.

J. Wagenaar, "Crossing the Sea of Reeds (Exod 13-14) and the Jordan (Josh 3-4): A Priestly Framework for the Wilderness Wandering," in: M. Vervenne (ed.), *Studies in the Book of Exodus*, Leuven 1996, 461-70.

237 S. Segert, "Crossing the Waters: Moses and Hamilcar," *JNES* 53 (1994), 195-203.

238 Th. B. Dozeman, *God at War: Power in the Exodus Tradition*, New York/Oxford 1996.

240 G.I. Davies, "Some Points of Interest in Sixteenth-Century Translations of Exodus 15," in: W. Horbury (ed.), *Hebrew Study from Ezra to Ben-Yehuda*, Edinburgh 1999, 249-56.

Th. B. Dozeman, "The Song of the Sea and Salvation History," in: S.L. Cook, S.C. Winter, *On the Way to Nineveh* (FS G.M. Landes), Atlanta, GA 1999, 94-113.

G. Fischer, "Das Schilfmeerlied Exodus 15 in seinem Kontext," *Bib* 77 (1996), 32-47.

J.P. Fokkelman, *Major Poems of the Hebrew Bible: At the Interface of Hermeneutics and Structural Analysis. I: Ex. 15, Deut. 32, and Job 3*, Assen 1998.

R.D. Patterson, "The Song of Redemption," *WthJ* 57 (1995), 453-61.

R.J. Tournay, "Le chant de victoire d'Exode 15," *RB* 102 (1995), 522-31.

243 W.J. Houston, "Misunderstanding or Midrash? The Prose Appropriation of Poetic Material in the Hebrew Bible (Part I)," *ZAW* 109 (1997), 342-55.

252 J.L. Kugel, *In Potiphar's House*, San Francisco 1990, 125-55 (on the Jewish tradition with regard to Joseph's bones).

254 W. Groß, "Die Wolkensäule und die Feuersäule in Ex 13 + 14: Literarkritische, redaktionsgeschichliche und quellenkritische Erwägungen," in: idem, *Studien zur Priesterschrift und zu alttestamentlichen Gottesbildern*, Stuttgart 1999, 97-122.

265 R. Hayward, "Some Ancient Jewish Reflections on Israel's Imminent Redemption," in: M.D. Caroll et al. (eds), *The Bible in Human Society*, Sheffield 1995, 293-305.

J. Maier, "Grundlage und Anwendung des Verbots der Rückkehr nach Ägypten," in: B. Kollmann et al. (eds), *Antikes Judentum und Frühes Christentum* (FS H. Stegemann), Berlin/New York 1999, 225-44.

M. Vervenne, "Topic and Comment: The Case of an Initial Superordinate אשר Clause in Exodus 14:13," in: E. Talstra (ed.), *Narrative and Comment* (FS W. Schneider), Amsterdam 1995, 187-98.

267 M. Vervenne, "Exodus 14,20 MT-LXX: Textual or Literary Variation?", in: J.-M. Auwers, A. Wénin (eds), *Lectures et relectures de la Bible* (FS P.-M. Bogaert), Leuven 1999, 3-25.

280 T. Giles, "The Chamberlain-Warren Samaritan Inscription CW 2472," *JBL* 114 (1996), 111-6 (on the text of Exod. 15:3, 11).

283 J.B. Bauer, "Wann heißt *'appayim* 'Zorn'? Ex 15,8; Prov. 30,33; Dan 11,20," *ZAW* 111 (1999), 92-4.

291 R. Kessler, "Gott und König, Grundeigentum und Fruchtbarkeit," *ZAW* 108 (1996), 214-32.

294 J. Braun, *Die Musikkultur Altisraels/Palästinas: Studien zu archäologischen, schriftlichen und vergleichenden Quellen*, Freiburg/Göttingen 1999.

Sh. O'Bryhim, "The Sphere-bearing Anthropomorphic Figurines of Amathus," *BASOR* 306 (1997), 39-45 (on women with hand drums).

A. Rebić, "Musik im Alten Testament," *Internationale Katholische Zeitschrift* 29 (2000), 296-304.

295 E.A. Knauf, "Supplementa Ismaelitica," *BN* 86 (1997), 49-50.

303 W. Johnstone, "From the Sea to the Mountain, Exodus 15,22-19,2: A Case Study in Editorial Techniques," in: M. Vervenne (ed.), *Studies in the Book of Exodus*, Leuven 1996, 245-63.

F.H. Polak, "Water, Rock and Wood: Structure and Thought Pattern in the Exodus Narrative," *JANES* 25 (1997), 19-42.

309 H. Avalos, *Illness and Health Care in the Ancient Near East: The Role of the Temple in Greece, Mesopotamia, and Israel*, Atlanta, GA 1995.

R. North, "Medicine and Healing in the Old Testament Background," in: idem, *Medicine in the Biblical Background and Other Essays on the Origins of Hebrew*, Rome 2000, 9-68.

320 P. Dumoulin, *Entre la manne et l'eucharistie: Étude de Sg 16,15-17,1a: La manne dans le livre de Sagesse, synthèse de traditions et préparation au mystère eucharistique*, Rom 1994.

355 J.A. Wagenaar, "The Cessation of Manna: Editorial Frames for the Wilderness Wandering in Exodus 16,35 and Joshua 5,10-12," *ZAW* 112 (2000), 192-209.

357 J.W. van Henten, "Judith as a Female Moses: Judith 7-13 in the Light of Exodus 17; Numbers 20 and Deuteronomy 33:8-11," in: F. van Dijk-Hemmes, A. Brenner (eds), *Reflections on Theology & Gender*, Kampen 1994, 33-48.

373 R. Dietzfelbinger, "Ex 17,8-16 in der frühchristlichen Exegese: Einige Anmerkungen," in: M. Vervenne (ed.), *Studies in the Book of Exodus*, Leuven 1996, 603-7.

O. Keel, "Powerful Symbols of Victory – The Parts Stay the Same, the Actors Change," *JNSL* 25 (1999), 205-40.

E.A. Rooze, *Amalek geweldig verslagen: Een bijbels-theologisch onderzoek naar de vijandschap Israël-Amalek als bijdrage tot de discussie over 'geweld in het Oude Testament'*, Gorinchem 1995.

A. Sagi, "The Punishment of Amalek in Jewish Tradition: Coping with the Moral Problem," *HThR* 87 (1994), 323-46.

A. Schuil, *Amalek: Onderzoek naar oorsprong en ontwikkeling van Amaleks rol in het Oude Testament*, Zoetermeer 1997.

396 E. Carpenter, "Exodus 18: Its Structure, Style, Motifs and Function in the Book of Exodus," in: E.E. Carpenter (ed.), *A Biblical Itinerary: In Search of Method, Form and Content* (FS G.W. Coats), Sheffield 1997, 91-108.

S.L. Cook, "The Tradition of Mosaic Judges: Past Approaches and New Directions," in: S.L. Cook, S.C. Winter, *On the Way to Nineveh* (FS G.M. Landes), Atlanta, GA 1999, 286-315.

A. Graupner, "Exodus 18,13-27 – Ätiologie einer Justizreform in Israel?" in: S. Beyerle et al. (eds), *Recht und Ethos im Alten Testament – Gestalt und Wirkung* (FS H. Seebass), Neukirchen-Vluyn 1991, 11-26.

E.L. Greenstein, "Jethro's Wit: An Interpretation of Wordplay in Exodus 18," in: S.L. Cook, S.C. Winter, *On the Way to Nineveh* (FS G.M. Landes), Atlanta, GA 1999, 155-71.

G. Harkam, "'Die Sache ist dir zu schwer ...' Das Entlastungsmotiv in Ex 18:23-27 und das Modell von 'Management by Concentration and Delegation'," in: J.A. Loader, H.V. Kieweiler (eds.), *Vielseitigkeit des Alten Testaments* (FS G. Sauer), Frankfurt etc. 1999, 49-61.

C. Houtman, "Autoritative Interpretation im Deuteronomium: Beleuchtet anhand von Deuteronomium 1:9-18," in: J.W. Dyk et al. (eds), *Unless Some One Guide Me...* (FS K.A. Deurloo), Maastricht 2001, 57-65.

398 F. Crüsemann, "Das Bundesbuch – historischer Ort und institutioneller Hintergrund," *SVT* 40 (1988), 27-41.

G.N. Knoppers, "Jehoshaphat's Judiciary and 'The Scroll of YHWH's Torah'," *JBL* 113 (1994), 59-80.

418 P.J. Harland, "בצע: Bribe, Extortion or Profit?", *VT* 50 (2000), 310-22.

425 L. Teugels, "Did Moses See the Chariot? The Link between Exod 19-20 and Ezek 1 in Early Jewish Interpretation," in: M. Vervenne (ed.), *Studies in the Book of Exodus*, Leuven 1996, 595-602.

A. Wénin, "La théophanie au Sinaï: Structures littéraires et narration en Ex 19,10-20,21," in: M. Vervenne (ed.), *Studies in the Book of Exodus*, Leuven 1996, 471-80.

426 T.D. Alexander, "The Composition of the Sinai Narrative in Exodus XIX 1 – XXIV 11," *VT* 49 (1999), 1-20.

Y. Avishur, "The Narrative of the Revelation at Sinai (Exod 19-24)," in: G. Galil, M. Weinfeld (eds), *Studies in Historical Geography and Biblical Historiography* (FS Z. Kallai), Leiden etc. 2000, 197-214.

J. Blenkinsopp, "Deuteronomic Contributions to the Narrative in Genesis-Numbers," in: L.S. Schearing, S.L. McKenzie (eds), *Those Elusive Deuteronomists: The Phenomenon of Pan-Deuteronomism*, Sheffield 1999, 84-115.

J. Blenkinsopp, "Structure and Meaning in the Sinai-Horeb Narrative (Exodus 19-34)," in: E.E. Carpenter (ed.), *A Biblical Itinerary: In Search of Method, Form and Content* (FS G.W. Coats), Sheffield 1997, 109-25.

M.R. Hauge, *The Descent From the Mountain: Narrative Patterns in Exodus 19-40*, Sheffield 2001.

C. Houtman, "Der 'Tatian' des Pentateuch: Einheit und Kohärenz in Exodus 19-40," *EThL* 76 (2000), 381-95.

J.S. Kaminsky, "Paradise Regained: Rabbinic Reflections on Israel at Sinai," in: A. Ogden Bellis, J.S. Kaminsky (eds.), *Jews, Christians, and the*

Theology of the Hebrew Scriptures, Atlanta, GA 2000, 15-43.

A. Niccacci, "Narrative Syntax of Exodus 19-24," in: E. van Wolde (ed.), *Narrative Syntax and the Hebrew Bible*, Leiden etc. 1997, 203-28.

W. Oswald, *Israel am Gottesberg: Eine Untersuchung zur Literargeschichte der vorderen Sinaiperikope Ex 19-24 und deren historischen Hintergrund*, Freiburg/Göttingen 1998.

J. Van Seters, "Is There Evidence of a Dtr Redaction in the Sinai Pericope (Exodus 19-24, 32-34)?," in: L.S. Schearing, S.L. McKenzie (eds.), *Those Elusive Deuteronomists: The Phenomenon of Pan-Deuteronomism*, Sheffield 1999, 160-70.

B.D. Sommer, "Revelation at Sinai in the Hebrew Bible and in Jewish Theology," *JR* 79 (1999), 422-51.

E. Zenger, "Wie und wozu die Tora zum Sinai kam: Literarische und theologische Beobachtungen zu Exodus 19-34," in: M. Vervenne (ed.), *Studies in the Book of Exodus*, Leuven 1996, 265-88.

429 A. Scriba, *Die Geschichte des Motivkomplexes Theophanie: Seine Elemente, Einbindung in Geschehensabläufe und Verwendungsweisen in altisraelitischer, frühjüdischer und frühchristlicher Literatur*, Göttingen 1995.

442 R. Kasher, "Metaphor and Allegory in the Aramaic Translations of the Bible," *Journal of the Aramaic Bible* 1 (1999), 53-77.

445 H. Jagersma, "Structure and Function of Exodus 19:3bβ-6," in: J.W. Dyk et al. (eds), *Unless Some One Guide Me...* (FS K.A. Deurloo), Maastricht 2001, 43-48.

R. Mosis, "Ex 19,5b.6a: Syntaktischer Aufbau und lexikalische Semantik," in: idem, *Gesammelte Aufsätze zum Alten Testament*, Würzburg 1999, 119-149.

A. Schenker, "'Ein Königreich von Priestern' (Ex 19,6): Welche Priester sind gemeint?", *IKZ* 25 (1996), 483-90.

A. Schenker, "Drei Mosaiksteinen: 'Königreich von Priestern', 'Und ihre Kinder gehen weg', 'Wir tun und wir hören' (Exodus 19,6; 21,22; 24,7)," in: M. Vervenne (ed.), *Studies in the Book of Exodus*, Leuven 1996, 367-80.

L. Schmidt, "Israel und das Gesetz: Ex 19,3b-8 und 24,3-8 als literarischer und theologischer Rahmen für das Bundesbuch," *ZAW* 113 (2001), 167-85.

J.L. Ska, "Exode 19,3b-6 et l'identité de l'Israël postexilique," in: M. Vervenne (ed.), *Studies in the Book of Exodus*, Leuven 1996, 289-317.

G. Steins, "Priesterherrschaft, Volk von Priestern oder was? Zur Interpretation von Ex 19,6," *BZ* 45 (2001), 20-36.

454 M. Wilcox, "'Silence in Heaven' (Rev 8:1) and Early Jewish Thought," in: Z.J. Kapera (ed.), *Mogilany 1989: Papers on the Dead Sea Scrolls in Memory of Jean Carmignac*, Part 2, Cracow 1991, 241-44.

455 B. Gosse, "Exodus 19,18 in the Biblical Redaction," in: K.-D. Schunck, M. Augustin (eds), *'Lasset uns Brücken bauen ...': Collected Communications to the XVth Congress of the Organization for the Study of the Old Testament, Cambridge 1995*, Frankfurt am Main etc. 1998, 41-3.

Additions to Volume 3

1   A. Graupner, "Vom Sinai zum Horeb oder vom Horeb zum Sinai? Zur Intention der Doppelüberlieferungen des Dekalogs," in: idem et al. (eds), *Verbindungslinien* (FS W.H. Schmidt), Neukirchen-Vluyn 2000, 85-101.
     S. Sekine, "The Ten Commandments: An Old Testament-Based Exegesis and Their Ethical Grounds," in: idem, *Transcendency and Symbols in the Old Testament: A Genealogy of the Hermeneutical Experiences*, Berlin/New York 1999, 16-90.
     R.E. Tapy, "The Code of Kinship in the Ten Commandments," *RB* 107 (2000), 321-37.
     S. Timm, "Der Heilige Mose bei den Christen Ägyptens: Eine Skizze zur Nachgeschichte alttestamentlicher Texte," in: *Religion im Erbe Ägyptens – Beiträge zur spätantiken Religionsgeschichte* (FS A. Böhlig), Wiesbaden 1988, 197-220.

18   J. Assmann, "Monotheismus und Ikonoklasmus als politische Theologie," in: E. Otto (ed.), *Mose: Ägypten und das Alte Testament*, Stuttgart 2000, 121-39.
     B. Becking et al., *Only One God? Monotheism in Ancient Israel and the Veneration of the Goddess Asherah*, Sheffield 2001.
     A. Berlejung, "Geheimnis und Ereignis: Zur Funktion und Aufgabe der Kultbilder in Mesopotamien," *Jahrbuch für Biblische Theologie* 13 (1998), 31-51.
     A. Berlejung, "Ikonophobie oder Ikonolatrie: Zur Auseinandersetzung um die Bilder im Alten Testament," in: B. Janowski, M. Köckert (eds), *Religionsgeschichte Israels: Formale und materiale Aspekte*, Gütersloh 1999, 208-41.
     A. Berlejung, *Die Theologie der Bilder: Herstellung und Einweihung von Kultbildern in Mesopotamien und die alttestamentliche Bilderpolemik*, Freiburg/Göttingen 1999.
     P. Eschweiler, *Bildzauber im alten Ägypten: Die Verwendung von Bildern und Gegenständen in magischen Handlungen nach den Texten des Mittleren und Neuen Reiches*, Freiburg/Göttingen 1994.
     M.D. Dick (ed.), *Born in Heaven, Made on Earth: The Making of the Cult Image in the Ancient Near East*, Winona Lake, IN 1999.
     R.K. Gnuse, *No Other Gods: Emergent Monotheism in Israel*, Sheffield 1997.
     G. Kaiser, "War der Exodus der Sündenfall? Fragen an Jan Assmann anläßlich seiner Monographie 'Moses der Ägypter'," *ThZ* 98 (2001), 1-24 [on Jan Assmann's tendency to disparage monotheism].

K. Koch, "Monotheismus als Sündenbock?," *ThLZ* 124 (1999), 874-84.

B. Lang, "Der eine Gott im Weltbild der Bibel: Ein Versuch den Monotheismus zu verstehen," in: A. Hölscher, R. Kampling (eds), *Glauben in Welt*, Berlin 1999, 9-28.

J. Pakkala, *Intolerant Monolatry in the Deuteronomistic History*, Helsinki/Göttingen 1999.

W.H.C. Propp, "Monotheism and 'Moses': The Problem of Early Israelite Religion," *UF* 31 (1999), 537-75.

H. Rechenmacher, *'Außer mir gibt es keinen Gott!': Eine sprach- und literaturwissenschaftliche Studie zur Ausschließlichkeitsformel*, St. Ottilien 1997.

A. Schart, "Die 'Gestalt' YHWHs: Ein Beitrag zur Körpermataphorik alttestamentlicher Rede von Gott," *ThZ* 55 (1999), 26-43.

W.H. Schmidt, "Das erste Gebot als prägende Kraft," in: *Hören und Lernen in der Schule des NAMENS* (FS B. Klappert), Neukirchen-Vluyn 1999, 26-40.

26 J. Krašovec, *Reward, Punishment, and Forgiveness: The Thinking and Beliefs of Ancient Israel in the Light of Greek and Modern Views*, Leiden etc. 1999, 110-59.

H. Graf Reventlow, "Ezechiel 18,1-20: Eine Mutmachende prophctische Botschaft für unsere Zeit," in: S. Beyerle et al. (eds), *Recht und Ethos im Alten Testament – Gestalt und Wirkung* (FS H. Seebass), Neukirchen-Vluyn 1991, 155-65.

H.J. Korevaar, "To Which Family Do You Belong? Parallel Family Structures in the Second Commandment (Ex 20:5b-6)," *OTE* 12 (1999), 279-97.

K. Schmid, "Kollektivschuld? Der Gedanke übergreifender Schuldzusamenhänge im Alten Testament und im Alten Orient," *ZABR* 5 (1999), 193-222.

32 J.E. Wright, "Biblical Versus Israelite Images of the Heavenly Realm," *JSOT* 93 (2001), 59-75.

34 P. Sanders, "Toen zei David: God verdoeme mij ...," *NedThT* 55 (2001), 286-300.

39 V. Nikiprowetzky,"Le sabbat et les armes dans l'histoire ancienne d'Israël," *REJ* 159 (2000), 1-17.

I. Willi-Plein, "Anmerkungen zu Wortform und Semantik des Sabbat," *ZAH* 10 (1997), 201-6.

49 T.H. Blomquist, *Gates and Gods: Cults in the City Gates of Iron Age Palestine – An Investigation of the Archaeological and Biblical Sources*, Stockholm 1999.

51 M. Millard, "Das Elterngebot im Dekalog: Zum Problem der Gliederung des Dekalogs'," in: E. Blum (ed.), *Mincha* (FS R. Rendtorff), Neukirchen-Vluyn 2000, 193-216.

55 L. Lanner, "Cannibal Mothers and Me: A Mother's Reading of 2 Kings 6.24-7.20," *JSOT* 85 (1999), 107-16.

58 A. Schüle, "'Denn er ist wie du': Zu Übersetzung und Verständnis des alttestamentlichen Liebesgebots Lev 19,18," *ZAW* 113 (2001), 515-34.

80 H.A. Hoffner, *The Laws of the Hittites: A Critical Edition*, Leiden 1997.

88 A. Fitzpatrick-McKinley, *The Transformation of Torah from Scribal Advice to Law*, Sheffield 1999.

H. Hoffmann, *Das Gesetz in der frühjüdischen Apokalyptik*, Göttingen1999.

B.S. Jackson, "'Law' and 'Justice' in the Bible," *JJS* 49 (1998), 218-29.

93 J.W. Watts, "The Legal Characterization of God in the Pentateuch," *HUCA* 67 (1996), 1-14.

95 K. Grünwaldt, *Das Heiligkeitsgesetz Leviticus 17-26: Ursprüngliche Gestalt, Tradition und Theologie*, Berlin/New York 1999.

J. Joosten, "Moïse a-t-il recelé le Code de Sainteté?", *BN* 84 (1996), 75-86.

J. Joosten, *People and Land in te Holiness Code: An Exegetical Study of the Ideational Framework of the Law in Leviticus 17-26*, Leiden etc. 1996.

H.-W. Jüngling, "Das Buch Levitikus in der Forschung seit Karl Elligers Kommentar aus dem Jahr 1966," in: H.-J. Fabry, H.-W. Jüngling (eds), *Levitikus als Buch*, Berlin etc. 1999, 1-45.

R.A. Kugler, "Holiness, Purity, the Body and Society: The Evidence for Theological Conflict in Leviticus," *JSOT* 76 (1997), 3-27.

B.M. Levinson, *Deuteronomy and the Hermeneutics of Legal Innovation*, New York 1997.

E. Otto, *Das Deuteronomium*, Berlin/New York 1999.

E. Otto, *Das Deuteronomium im Pentateuch und Hexateuch*, Tübingen 2000.

J. Van Seters, "Cultic Laws in the Covenant Code and their Relationship to Deuteronomy and the Holiness Code," in: M. Vervenne (ed.), *Studies in the Book of Exodus*, Leuven 1996, 319-45.

K. Sparks, "A Comparative Study of the Biblical נבלה Laws," *ZAW* 110 (1998), 594-600.

J.W. Watts, *Reading Law: The Rhetorical Shaping of the Pentateuch*, Sheffield 1999.

96 A. Biedenkopf-Ziehner, "Ethische Forderungen im paganen und christlichen Ägypten, " *Göttinger Miszellen* 162 (1998), 25-37.

99 P. Heger, *The Three Biblical Altar Laws: Developments in the Sacrificial Cult in Practice and Theology, Political and Economic Background*, Berlin/New York 1999.

J. Milgrom, "Does H Advocate the Centralization of Worship?," *JSOT* 88 (2000), 59-76.

N. Na'aman, "The Law of the Altar in Deuteronomy and the Cultic Site Near Schechem", in: S.L. McKenzie, Th. Römer (eds), *Rethinking the*

Foundations: Historiography in the Ancient World and in the Bible (FS J. Van Seters), Berlin/New York 2000), 141-61.

Th. C. Römer, "Du Temple au Livre: L'idéologie de la centralisation dans l'historiographie deutéronomiste," in: S.L. McKenzie, Th. Römer (eds), *Rethinking the Foundations: Historiography in the Ancient World and in the Bible* (FS J. Van Seters), Berlin/New York 2000), 207-25.

J. Schaper, "Schriftauslegung und Schriftwerdung im alten Israel: Eine vergleichende Exegese von Ex 20,24-26 und Dtn 12,13-19," *ZABR* 5 (1999), 111-32.

110 C. Carmichael, "The Three Laws on the Release of Slaves (Ex 21,2-11; Dtn 15,12-18; Lev 25,39-46)," *ZAW* 112 (2000), 509-25.

E. Otto, "Soziale Restitution und Vertragsrecht: *mišaru(m), (an)-durāru(m), kirenzi, parā tarnumar, šᵉmiṭṭa* und *ḍ rôr* in Mesopotamien, Syrien, in der hebräischen Bibel und die Frage des Rechtstransfers im Alten Orient," *RA* 92 (1998), 125-60.

113 M. Bar-Ilan, *Some Jewish Women in Antiquity*, Atlanta, GA 1998.

G. Braulik, "Durften auch Frauen in Israel Opfern? Beobachtungen zur Sinn- und Festgestalt des Opfers im Deuteronomium," *Liturgisches Jahrbuch* 48 (1998), 222-48.

H. Jahnow et al., *Feministische Hermeneutik und Erstes Testament: Analysen und Interpretationen*, Stuttgart 1994.

S. Lafont, *Femmes, droit et justice dans l'Antiquité orientale: Contributions à l'étude du droit pénal au Proche-Orient ancien*, Fribourg/Göttingen 1999.

I. Ljung, *Silence or Suppression: Attitudes towards Women in the Old Testament*, Stockholm 1989.

C. Pressler, "Wives and Daughters, Bond and Free: Views of Women in the Slave Laws of Exodus Exodus 21.2-11," in: V.H. Matthews et al. (eds), *Gender and Law in the Hebrew Bible and the Ancient Near East*, Sheffield 1998, 147-72.

E. Seifert, *Tochter und Vater im Alten Testament: Eine ideologiekritische Untersuchung zur Verfügungsgewalt von Vätern über ihre Töchter*, Neukirchen-Vluyn 1997.

I. Tal, *Integrating Women into Second Temple History*, Tübingen 1999.

R. Westbrook, "The Female Slave," in: V.H. Matthews et al. (eds), *Gender and Law in the Hebrew Bible and the Ancient Near East*, Sheffield 1998, 214-38.

F. Zéman, "Le statut de la femme en Mésopotamie," *ScEs* 43 (1991), 69-86.

121 S. Greengus, "The Selling of Slaves: Laws Missing from the Hebrew Bible," *ZABR* 3 (1997), 1-11.

123 M. Anbar, "La libération des esclaves en temps de guerre: Jer 34 et ARM XXVI.363," *ZAW* 111 (1999), 253-55.

124 H.-J. Fabry, "Deuteronomium 15: Gedanken zur Geschwister-Ethik im Al-

ten Testament," *ZABR* 3 (1997), 92-111.

E.L. Gibson, *The Jewish Manumission Inscriptions of The Bosporus Kingdom*, Tübingen 1999.

P.J. Olivier, "Restitution as Economic Redress: The Fine Print of the Old Babylonian *mēšarum*-Edict of Ammiṣaduqa," *ZABR* 3 (1997), 12-25 (also published in *JNSL* 24 [1998], 83-99).

M.J. Oosthuizen, "Deuteronomy 15:1-18 in Socio-Rhetorical Perspective," *ZABR* 3 (1997), 64-91.

E. Otto, "Programme der sozialen Gerechtigkeit: Die neuassyrische *(an)durāru*-Institution sozialen Ausgleichs und das deuteronomische Erlaßjahr in Dtn 15," *ZABR* 3 (1997), 26-63.

130 E. Levine, "On Exodus 21,10 *'Onah* and Biblical Marriage," *ZABR* 5 (1999), 133-64.

131 M. Anbar, "L'influence deutéronomique sur le Code de l'Alliance: Le cas d'Exode 21:12-17," *ZABR* 5 (1999), 165-66.

B. Gosse, "Subversion de la législation du Pentateuque et symboliques respectives des lignées de David et de Saül dans les livres de Samuel et de Ruth," *ZAW* 110 (1998), 34-49.

A. Schenker, "Die Analyse der Intentionalität im Bundesbuch (Ex 21-23)," *ZABR* 4 (1998), 209-17 (also published in *JNSL* 24 [1998], 1-12).

167 R. Haase, "Talion und spiegelnde Strafe in den keilschriftlichen Rechtscorpora," *ZABR* 3 (1977), 195-210.

J. Van Seters, "Some Observations on the *Lex Talionis* in Exod 21:23-25," in: S. Beyerle et al. (eds), *Recht und Ethos im Alten Testament – Gestalt und Wirkung* (FS H. Seebass), Neukirchen-Vluyn 1991, 27-37.

Y. Shemesh, "'Measure for Measure' in Biblical Law, Compared to the Law of the Ancient Near East and Bedouin Law," *BetM* 45 (2000), 146-67.

169 A. Schenker, "Drei Mosaiksteinen: 'Königreich von Priestern', 'Und ihre Kinder gehen weg', 'Wir tun und wir hören' (Exodus 19,6; 21,22; 24,7)," in: M. Vervenne (ed.), *Studies in the Book of Exodus*, Leuven 1996, 367-80.

185 A. Schenker, "La différence des peines pour les vols de bétail selon le *Code de l'Alliance* (Ex XX,37 et XII,3)," *RB* 107 (2000), 18-23.

196 H.J. Boecker, "Überlegungen zur sogenannten Familiengerichtsbarkeit in der Frühgeschichte Israels," in: S. Beyerle et al. (eds), *Recht und Ethos im Alten Testament – Gestalt und Wirkung* (FS H. Seebass), Neukirchen-Vluyn 1991, 3-9.

E. Otto, "Diachronie und Synchronie im Depositenrecht des 'Bundesbuches': Zur jüngsten literatur- und rechtshistorischen Diskussion von Ex 22, 6-14," *ZABR* 2 (1996), 76-85.

207 T. Frymer-Kensky, "Virginity in the Bible" in: V.H. Matthews et al. (eds), *Gender and Law in the Hebrew Bible and the Ancient Near East*, Sheffield 1998, 97-112.

216 W. Fleckenstein, "Einen Fremden sollst du nicht ausnützen oder ausbeuten," *MTZ* 48 (1997), 1-8.

220 E. Bons, "Konnte eine Witwe die *naḥᵃlāh* ihres verstorbenen Mannes erben? Überlegungen zum Ostrakon 2 aus der Sammlung Moussaïeff," *ZABR* 4 (1998), 197-208.

H.J. Boecker, "'Feindesliebe' im alttestamentlichen Recht? Überlegungen zu Ex 23, 4-5," in A. Graupner et al. (eds), *Verbindungslinien* (FS W.H. Schmidt), Neukirchen-Vluyn 2000, 19-25.

247 U. Berges, "Die Armen im Buch Jesaja: Ein Beitrag zur Literaturgeschichte des AT.," *Bib* 80 (1999), 153-77.

U. Berges, "Armoede en haar bestrijding in de wetten van het Oude Testament," *TvT* 40 (2000), 227-50.

251 W. Groß, "Die alttestamentlichen Gesetze zu Brach-, Sabbat-, Erlaß- und Jubeljahr und Zinsverbot," *ThQ* 180 (2000), 1-15.

E. Otto, "Soziale Restitution und Vertragsrecht: *mišaru(m), (an)-durāru(m), kirenzi, parā tarnumar, šᵉmiṭṭa* und *dᵉrôr* in Mesopotamien, Syrien, in der hebräischen Bibel und die Frage des Rechtstransfers im Alten Orient," *RA* 92 (1998), 125-60.

A. Schenker, "Der Boden und seine Produktivität im Sabbat- und Jubeljahr: Das *dominium terrae* in Ex 23,10f und Lev 25,2-12," in: H.-P. Mathys (ed.), *Ebenbild Gottes – Herrscher über die Welt*, Neukirchen-Vluyn 1998, 94-106.

G. Scheuermann (ed.), *Das Jobeljahr im Wandel: Untersuchungen zu Erlaß- und Jobeljahrtexten aus vier Jahrtausenden*, Würzburg 2000.

260 D.E. Fleming, "The Israelite Festival Calendar and Emar's Ritual Archive," *RB* 106 (1999), 8-34.

D.E. Fleming, "A Break in the Line: Reconsidering the Bible's Festival Calendars," *RB* 106 (1999), 161-74.

C. Körting, *Der Schall des Schofar: Israels Fests im Herbst*, Berlin/New York 1999.

273 H. Ausloos, "Deuteronomi(sti)c Elements in Exod 23, 20-33?", in: M. Vervenne (ed.), *Studies in the Book of Exodus*, Leuven 1996, 481-500.

H. Ausloos, "The Risks of Rash Textual Criticism Illustrated on the Basis of the *Numeruswechsel* in Exod 23, 20-33," *BN* 97 (1999), 5-12.

H. Ausloos, "Exod 23,20-33 and the 'War of YHWH'," *Bib* 80 (1999), 555-63.

Y. Hoffmann, "The Deuteronomistic Concept of the Herem," *ZAW* 111 (1999), 196-210.

284 M. Anbar, "Deux cérémonies d'alliance dans Ex 24 à la lumière des archives royales de Mari," *UF* 30 (1998), 1-4.

J.W. Hilber, "Theology of Worship in Exodus 24," *JETS* 39 (1996), 177-89.

291 A. Schenker, "Drei Mosaiksteinen: 'Königreich von Priestern', 'Und ihre

Kinder gehen weg', 'Wir tun und wir hören' (Exodus 19,6; 21,22; 24,7)," in: M. Vervenne (ed.), *Studies in the Book of Exodus*, Leuven 1996, 367-80.

306 E. Cortese, "The Priestly Tent (Ex 25-31.35-40): Literary Criticism and Theology of P," *Liber Annuus Studii Biblici Franciscani* 48 (1998), 9-30.

D.E. Fleming, "Mari's Large Public Tent and the Priestly Tent Sanctuary," *VT* 50 (2000), 484-98.

R.E. Longacre, "Building for the Worship of God," in: W.R. Bodine (ed.), *Discourse Analysis of Biblical Literature: What it is and What it Offers*, Atlanta, GA 1995, 21-49.

R.A. Rapport, *Ritual and Religion in the Making of Humanity*, Cambridge 1999.

318 A.M. Cooper, B.R. Goldstein, "At the Entrance to the Tent: More Cultic Resonances in Biblical Narrative," *JBL* 116 (1997), 201-15.

336 J. Bär, *Der assyrische Tribut und seine Darstellung: Eine Untersuchung zur imperialen Ideologie im neuassyrischen Reich*, Kevelaer/Neukirchen-Vluyn 1996.

366 S. Van Den Eynde, "Chronicler's Usage of the Collocation ארון ברית יהוה," *ZAW* 113 (2001), 422-30.

M. Görg, "Die Lade als Sarg: Zur Traditionsgeschichte von Bundeslade und Josefssarg," *BN* 105 (2000), 5-11.

C. Schäfer-Lichtenberger, "'Sie wird nicht wieder hergestellt werden': Anmerkungen zum Verlust der Lade," in: E. Blum (ed.), *Mincha* (FS R. Rendtorff), Neukirchen-Vluyn 2000, 229-42.

380 J. Gutmann, "The Strange History of the *Kapporet* Ritual," *ZAW* 112 (2000), 624-6.

400 E. Talstra, "Reconstructing the *menorah* on Disk: Some Syntactic Remarks," in: M. Vervenne (ed.), *Studies in the Book of Exodus*, Leuven 1996, 523-33.

493 C. Batsch et al. (eds.), *Zwischen Krise und Alltag: Antike Religionen im Mittelmeerraum*, Stuttgart 1999 (C. Batsch on the urim and tummim in second temple Judaism).

A.M. Kitz, "The Hebrew Terminology of Lot Casting and Its Ancient Near Eastern Context," *CBQ* 62 (2000), 207-14.

A.M. Kitz, "Undivided Inheritance and Lot Casting in the Book of Joshua," *JBL* 119 (2000), 601-18.

E. Noort, "Numbers 27,21: The Priestly Oracle Urim and Tummim and the History of Reception," in: H.L.J. Vanstiphout et al. (eds), *All Those Nation ...Cultural Encounters within and with the Near East* (FS Han Drijvers), Groningen 1999, 109-16.

495 H.B. Huffmon, "Priestly Divination in Israel," in: C.L. Meyers, M. O'Connor (eds), *The Word of the Lord Shall Go Forth* (FS D.N. Freedman), Winona Lake, IN 1983, 355-59.

517 S.D. Sperling, "Pants, Persians, and the Priestly Source," in: R. Chazan et al. (eds), *Ki Baruch Hu: Ancient Near Eastern, Biblical and Judaic Studies* (FS B.A. Levine), Winona Lake, IN 1999, 373-85.

524 D. Fleming, "The Biblical Tradition of Anointing Priests," *JBL* 117 (1998), 401-14.

569 E.L. Greenstein, "Recovering 'the Women Who Served at the Entrance," in: G. Galil, M. Weinfeld (eds), *Studies in Historical Geography and Biblical Historiography* (FS Z. Kallai), Leiden etc. 2000, 165-73.

579 I.D. Ritchie, "The Nose Knows: Bodily Knowing in Isaiah 11.3," *JSOT* 87 (2000), 59-73.

588 W. Groß, "Der neue Bund in Jer 31 und die Suche nach übergreifenden Bundeskonzeptionen im Alten Testament," *Theologische Quartalschrift* 176 (1996), 259-72.
J.T.A.G.M. van Ruiten, "The Relationship between Exod 31, 12-17 and Jubilees 2,1.17-33," in: M. Vervenne (ed.), *Studies in the Book of Exodus*, Leuven 1996, 567-75.

605 K. Koenen, "Eherne Schlange und goldenes Kalb," *ZAW* 111 (1999), 353-72.
J. Krašovec, *Reward, Punishment, and Forgiveness: The Thinking and Beliefs of Ancient Israel in the Light of Greek and Modern Views*, Leiden etc. 1999, 84-109.
B. Renaud, *L'Alliance, un mystère de miséricorde: Une lecture de Exode 32-34*, Paris 1998.

616 C. Begg, "The Golden Calf Episode According to Pseudo-Philo," in: M. Vervenne (ed.), *Studies in the Book of Exodus*, Leuven 1996, 577-94.
B.N. Fisk, "Scripture Shaping Scripture: The Interpretive Role of Biblical Citations in Pseudo-Philo's Episode of the Golden Calf," *JSP* 17 (1998), 3-23.
H.-C. Schmitt, "Die Erzählung vom goldenen Kalb Ex 32 und das deuteronomistische Geschichtswerk," in: S.L. McKenzie, Th. Römer (eds), *Rethinking the Foundations: Historiography in the Ancient World and in the Bible* (FS J. Van Seters), Berlin/New York 2000), 235-50.

629 L. Brisman, "Sacred Butchery: Exodus 32:25-29,": in C. Seitz et al. (eds), *Theological Exegesis* (FS B.S. Childs), Grand Rapis, MI/Cambridge, U.K. 1999), 162-81.

634 V.A. Hurowitz, "Who Lost an Earring? Genesis 35:4 Reconsidered," *CBQ* 62 (2000), 28-32.

652 U. Becker, "Der Prophet als Fürbitter: Zum literarhistorischen Ort der Amos-Visionen," *VT* 51 (2001), 141-65.

659 G.J. Venema, "Why Did Moses Destroy 'The Golden Calf'? Four Readings of Deuteronomy 9:21 and Exodus 32:20," in: J.W. Dyk et al. (eds), *The Rediscovery of the Hebrew Bible*, Maastricht 1999, 39-49.

682 G. Barbiero, "Ex. xxxiii 7-11: Eine synchrone Lektüre," *VT* 50 (2000), 154-66.

F.-L. Hossfeld, "Das Privilegrecht Ex 34,11-26 in der Diskussion," in: S. Beyerle et al. (eds), *Recht und Ethos im Alten Testament – Gestalt und Wirkung* (FS H. Seebass), Neukirchen-Vluyn 1991, 39-59.

711 D.F. O'Kennedy, "'And It Shall Be Forgiven Him/Them': The Concept of Forgiveness in the Pentateuch," *OTE* 12 (1999), 94-113.

U. Kellermann, "Wer kann Sünden vergeben außer Elia?" in: P. Mommer et al. (eds), *Gottes Recht und Lebensraum* (FS H.J. Boecker), Neukirchen-Vluyn 1993, 165-77.

S. von Sonke, *Der betende Sünder vor Gott: Studien zu Vergebungs-vorstellungen in urchristlichen und frühjüdischen Texten*, Leiden etc. 1999

716 R.M. Alonso García, "Ex 34,10-28: Un estudio histórico-literario," *EstBib* 56 (1998), 433-64.

731 B. Dozeman, "Masking Moses and Mosaic Authority in Torah," *JBL* 199 (2000), 21-45.

735 J.A. Beck, *Translators as Storytellers: A study in Septuagint Translation Techniques*, New York 2000.

N. Fernández Marcos, *The Septuagint in Context: Introduction to the Greek Versions of the Bible*, Leiden etc. 2000.

HISTORICAL COMMENTARY ON THE OLD TESTAMENT

PUBLISHED VOLUMES

Exodus I: Exodus 1:1-7:13 (1993)   Cornelis Houtman, Kampen, The Netherlands
Exodus II: Exodus 7:14-19:25 (1996) Cornelis Houtman, Kampen, The Netherlands
Exodus III: Exodus 20-40 (2000)   Cornelis Houtman, Kampen, The Netherlands
Exodus IV: Supplement (2002)   Cornelis Houtman, Kampen, The Netherlands
1 Kings I/1: 1 Kings 1-11 (1998)   Martin J. Mulder†, Leiden, The Netherlands
Isaiah II/2: Isaiah 28-39 (2000)   Willem A.M.Beuken, Leuven, Belgium
Isaiah III/1: Isaiah 40-48 (1997)   Jan L. Koole†, Kampen, The Netherlands
Isaiah III/2: Isaiah 49-55 (1998)   Jan L. Koole†, Kampen, The Netherlands
Isaiah III/3: Isaiah 56-66 (2001)   Jan L. Koole†, Kampen, The Netherlands
Lamentations (1998)   Johan Renkema, Kampen, The Netherlands
Nahum (1997)   Klaas Spronk, Kampen, The Netherlands
Zephaniah (1999)   Johannes Vlaardingerbroek, Rotterdam, The Netherlands

FORTHCOMING VOLUMES

Habakuk   Gert T.M. Prinsloo, Pretoria, South Africa
Obadaiah   Johan Renkema, Kampen, The Netherlands
Song of Songs   Wilfred G.E. Watson, New Castle, England

PROJECTED VOLUMES

Genesis   Erhard Blum, Augsburg, Germany
Leviticus   James W. Watts, Hastings, Nebraska U.S.A.
Numbers   Frank A. Gosling, Sheffield, England
Deuteronomy   Cornelis Houtman, Kampen, The Netherlands
Joshua   Hartmut Rösel, Haifa, Israel
Judges   Klaas Spronk, Kampen, The Netherlands
Ruth   Marjo C.A. Korpel, Utrecht, The Netherlands
1 Samuel   Åke Viberg, Lund, Sweden
2 Samuel   Jichan Kim, Seoul, Korea
1 Kings 12-22   Jurie le Roux, Pretoria, South Africa
2 Kings   Kevin J. Cathcart, Dublin, Ireland
1 Chronicles   Peter B. Dirksen, Leiden, The Netherlands
2 Chronicles   Isaac Kalimi, Jerusalem, Israel
Ezra   Bob E.J.H. Becking, Utrecht, The Netherlands
Nehemiah   Edward Noort, Groningen, The Netherlands

Esther	Marjo C.A. Korpel, Utrecht, The Netherlands
Job	Richard S. Hess, Denver, Colorado, U.S.A
Psalms	Phil.J. Botha & Gert T.M. Prinsloo, Pretoria, South Africa
Proverbs	James A. Loader, Vienna, Austria
Ecclesiastes	Anton Schoors, Louvain, Belgium
Isaiah 1-12	Hendrik Leene, Amsterdam, The Netherlands
Isaiah 13-27	Willem A.M.Beuken, Leuven, Belgium
Jeremiah	Ben J. Oosterhoff† & Erik Peels, Apeldoorn, The Netherlands
Ezekiel 1-24	Herrie F. van Rooy, Potchefstroom, South Africa
Ezekiel 25-48	Corrine Patton, Tallahassee, Florida, U.S.A.
Daniel	
Hosea	Dwight R. Daniels, Glendale, CA U.S.A.
Joel	Willem van der Meer, Kampen, The Netherlands
Amos	Meindert Dijkstra, Utrecht, The Netherlands
Jonah	Johannes H. Potgieter, Pretoria, South Africa
Micah	Johannes C. de Moor, Kampen, The Netherlands
Haggai	William Th. Koopmans, Peterborough, Ont. Canada
Zechariah	Al Wolters, Ancaster, Ont. Canada
Malachi	S.D. Snyman, Bloemfontein, South Africa